POPE JOHN PAUL II

A DICTIONARY OF HIS LIFE AND TEACHINGS

by Fr M O'Carroll CSSp

Published and Distributed by:-

J.M.J. Publications
P.O. Box 385
Belfast BT9 6RQ
Northern Ireland
Fax: (0232) 381596

Pope John Paul II
A Dictionary of His Life and Teaching

1994   1st Printing (Canada) - 10,000

See back for the addresses of distributors

FOREWORD

I have aimed, in the following pages, to survey the entire career of John Paul II, to single out the principal themes of his teaching. I hope thereby to help the reader to judge the total personality and achievement of this man. I have, from study of his words and deeds and due reflection formed my idea of him. I have done so with more than general knowledge of the Papacy, in its theological aspect and in its historical evolution in the present century. As a priest journalist I followed week by week from 1956 to 1974 the careers of Pius XII, John XXIII and Paul VI. I did some detailed research into the career of Pius XII, first in the course of a long controversy on the Jewish Holocaust, in the *Irish Times*, 1964, then with a view to my book, *Pius XII, Greatness Dishonoured*. As a history teacher in Blackrock College, I had to cast a wider net.

I find John Paul II distinctive, shining with splendour in the vast papal gallery, which has many similar lights. His origins, his background, his experience as a young man were such as to prepare him for an arduous career. He was born into a nation that has been staunch in the faith, cultured and genetically brave. He is strong. The reader will have much evidence to show that he is highly intelligent, that he was in character forged in bitter fires. He lived through the two most cruel tyrannies of modern times.

Men are often moulded by meaningful association with great personalities. Karol Wojtyla was fortunate to come into the immediate circle of the two greatest ecclesial personalities in twentieth century Polish history, Adam Cardinal Sapieha and Stefan Cardinal Wyszynski. He differed in family background from the former, many times a prince; in temperament and outlook from the latter. But with both the faith and the Church bound him inseparably and intuitively. He brought something of each to the throne of Peter: Sapieha embodied Polish defiance and invincible idealism during the Second World War; Wysznski carried the Church on his back through the stalinist years. Each knew the meaning of treachery in different directions. Each had to see war declared to free Poland from Nazi tyranny, then their country delivered by international treaties into stalinist tyranny. What has the Polish people not had to endure?

Out of such torment came to the Petrine ministry this man so deeply acquainted with the mystery of Mary, the Mother of God, so richly endowed with the gifts of the Spirit, who has made him his foremost witness in the history of the modern papacy: no Pope has spoken or written so much and so well on the Holy Spirit. He has become for those with the sense of divine things, the exemplar of enlightened devotion to the Holy Spirit.

My book does not give a complete narrative of the Pope's career, an exhaustive analysis of his thought and teaching. That will demand an immense work, which I may yet undertake. But I hope that I have shown the notable aspects of his life and teaching, what posterity will delay on, what future generations in the Church will assimilate and take as nourishment. No one of his stature and of his productive achievement could be rightly appreciated in his lifetime. It will take generations to reach a satisfactory estimate of the man, of his contribution to the life of the Church and to the well-being of mankind. Giants tower over their contemporaries and are recognised only in the perspective of the ages. John Paul II is a giant and he belongs to the ages.

I have not given systematic bibliographies as I have done in previous works which have appeared over my name. That will come later. My immediate aim is to help those who, like me, are loyal to John Paul II and want to have information relevant to their fidelity. We are a company and I shall welcome any suggestion from my fellow members as to future editions of the present book. I do give occasional reference to books or articles which they may find helpful. I wish them to know that I have had them in mind, that I have written my pages for them, that I count on their prayers to enable me to continue in a task which may be onerous, but which it is an honour to accomplish: service of Jesus Christ in the person of the one who represents him at the head of his Mystical Body, the Church.

19 March, Feast of St Joseph
Patron of the Church, Protector of the Second Vatican Council

Michael O'Carroll, CSSp

Note to the Reader: Any references in the text to *L'Ossevatore Romano* have been abbreviated to *OR*.

Dedication

This book is dedicated to His Holiness Pope John Paul II.

Ability, Intellectual

Assessment of the intellectual ability of John Paul II does not depend on his election as Pope, but on his literary and administrative work prior to this fact. He was fifty eight-years of age when he became Pope. He stated recently to an audience of Roman university students that his seminary training had been deficient (cf *Sapieha, Adam Cardinal*). With this handicap his productive output in the thirty-two years from his priestly ordination to the papal election was prodigious. He participated actively in Vatican II (qv), spoke eleven times; he served three Congregations in Rome and on Polish episcopal commissions, represented the country abroad, notably at the Eucharistic Congresses at Melbourne in 1973 and Philadelphia in 1976, visiting the Poles in exile; he was asked to contribute to theological or pastoral congresses and he was the Polish member on Paul VI's commission on population, the family and births. Such tasks were incidental to the administration of a large Catholic diocese (cf *Cracow*). Nothing impeded a continuous flow of articles to reviews and to the Catholic weekly edited by his friend Jerzy Turowicz, *Tygodnik Powszechny*.

For concrete evidence of this diverse writing one may note that soon after the papal election, the Pope's university, the Angelico, devoted an entire issue of its review, *Angelicum*, to an analysis of his thought; nine contributors dealt with different aspects of this work. A bibliography of important articles ran to 190 items; five books could be listed: *Love and Responsibility*; *Person and Action*; *Sign of Contradiction* (the text of his retreat lectures to the papal household, 1976); *Foundations of Renewal. A Treatise on the implementation of Vatican II* (qv); *Faith in the theology of St John* (his Roman doctorate thesis) with which should be taken his Polish academic thesis on Max Scheler.

A more complete list of all the Pope's writings was made in 1980, *Karol Wojtyla negli scritti*; it ran to 1490 items in seven languages. The linguistic variety continues in his discourses and writings since he became Pope. What of the contents? How much of all that he says and writes is his own personal composition? This question is asked about all the Popes. From a cast-off of one year of the *Insegnamenti*, (1980) which gives everything that issues from the Papacy orally or in writing, I concluded that the total volume in his case amounts annually to the equivalent of ten books of one hundred thousand words each. One man could not, with the additional load of pastoral activity a Pope must carry, produce so much. Much of it is strictly theological, and the Pope's expertise was in philosophy. But he has to oversee every phase of composition, the choice of subject, the approach to the subject, the precise contents of an address or written text. He must approve the final draft and he takes full responsibility for what it contains. The items which attract most attention are the Encyclicals (qv) and Apostolic Exhortations. It is scarcely helpful to look for possible collaborators in producing these documents. I have had information from one scholar resident in Rome that he has made a contribution. I leave it at that (cf *Veritatis Splendor*).

Is John Paul II conspicuous as an intellectual Pope? Unquestionably. The only one
to be compared with him in our century is Pius XII. But his published work prior
to election was restricted to a number of addresses and sermons. Pius XI had
published some historical monographs, not very extensive in appeal. John XXIII was
engaged on research into the episcopal visitations of St Charles Borromeo, again
without wide impact.

For further information: J Mac Dermot SJ, *The Thought of John Paul II*, Rome,
Gregorian University, 1993.

Africa

John Paul II has visited Africa more often than anywhere else, eleven times in all.
He summoned a special synod on the Church in Africa, the third of this kind - the
first was on Holland in 1980 and the second on Europe in 1991. There have been
so far eight ordinary general synods; the ninth will take place in October 1994 on
religious life.

The synod met in Rome, which gave John Paul II the opportunity of close contact
with its work. The magnitude of the assembly points to the greatest success story
in modern missionary history. When the convert Jew Francis Libermann joined
forces with the first Vicar Apostolic, Edward Barron, appointed to West Africa, then
a mapless territory, there were few if any Catholics in the continent. The date was
1841. Today there are over ninety million. Great names besides those mentioned
figure in the story, Blessed Anne Marie Javouhey, who reached the coast of Africa,
Cardinal Lavigerie, founder of the White Fathers, Bishop Shanahan, often styled
Nigeria's St Patrick - eight million Catholics to give the title meaning, Bishop Marion
Brésillac, founder of the Society for African Missions, Edel Quinn, noted lay apostle
in east Africa in the forties of the present century, Blessed Daniel Brottier, builder
of Dakar's Souvenir Africain.

The initial cost in human lives was enormous. Of Libermann's first seven
missionaries, all but one died soon after arrival on African soil. Bishop Marion
Brésillac, with his heroic band, all perished likewise.

From such sacrifice come the 200 Cardinals and bishops meeting in Rome with 20
religious and diocesan priests, and observers including 13 laywomen and 13 laymen.
There will be consciousness of native African religious institutes, of a possible
teaching mission of Africa to the universal subject. The great themes were
proclamation, inculturation, dialogue (with other Christians, with Muslims and
traditional religions) justice and peace, and the mass media. Inculturation was a
dominant concern.

Let us not forget the decisive opening moment. Bishop Barron consecrated all those in his jurisdiction to the Immaculate Heart of Mary, as did another of his confrères for east Africa some time later. It evokes the immense problem of Russia's return to the faith. It all redounds to the glory of God and Our Lady and to their faithful servant, John Paul II. Africa is represented beside him at the summit of Church government by two Cardinals, Gantin and Arinze.

Alliance of the Two Hearts

On 22 September, 1986 the Pope received in a special audience the participants in the International Symposium on the Alliance of the Hearts of Jesus and Mary, which had concluded its session in Fatima. His opening words were:

"I am pleased to welcome all of you who have taken part in the International Symposium on the Alliance of the Hearts of Jesus and Mary, that was held this past week in Fatima. I wish to greet in a special way Cardinal Sin, the President of your Symposium, and together with him all who were responsible for formulating and carrying out the specific plans of your week of theological study. The title of your Symposium was taken from my Angelus Address of 15 September, 1985 when I made reference to that 'admirable alliance of hearts' of the Son of God and of his Mother. We can indeed say that devotion to the Sacred Heart of Jesus and to the Immaculate Heart of Mary has been an important part of the '*sensus fidei*' of the People of God during recent centuries. These devotions seek to direct our attention to Christ and to the role of his Mother in the mystery of Redemption, and though distinct, they are interrelated by reason of the enduring relation of love that exists between the Son and his Mother."

The Pope went on to expound the basic theology of the important theme. He had sent a letter of encouragement to the symposium members, through Cardinal Sin. On the day of the audience he was offered the collected proceedings of the session, with a *votum* asking that he would deign to publish a papal text based on them. This did not appear opportune, as he was about to issue his Encyclical on Our Lady, *Redemptoris Mater*.

The event itself is in deep harmony with a continuing, deeply rooted trend and with a whole outlook which characterizes John Paul II's personality, with notable effects on his pastoral ministry. A steering committee was set up in 1985 on the initiative of Filipino Catholics, Cardinal Sin, Fr Catalino Arevalo, SJ (of the Pontifical Ateneo, Manila, theological adviser to the Hierarchy), and Howard Dee, just then appointed Ambassador to the Holy See by President Corazon Aquino; John Haffert of the Blue Army collaborated. The steering committee had the assistance of the

Pontifical Marian Academy - the president, Fr Paolo Melada, OFM chaired the meetings. A number of highly qualified theologians accepted invitations to participate. Research on the theme from Sacred Scripture through the ages down to our time established its validity and fruitfulness. In September of the following year, 1987, a public congress was held in Manila to communicate the ideas to the faithful, again with the encouragement of the Pope. The Filipinos have continued with similar meetings in different centres: Akita, Fatima; elsewhere the idea of the Two Hearts has been an inspiration in private prayer and piety and in assemblies. Howard Dee has published an instructive work on the subject and kindred ideas, *Mankind's Final Destiny*, Manila, 1992.

Anti-Pope, An

It will appear alarmist to some to talk or write about the possibility of an Anti-Pope. Better be alarmist and stave off the evil, than naive and complacent to let it grow unimpeded. There have been Anti-Popes in the past. Do things now appear to expose the faithful to such a happening? The answer to this question depends on the degree to which criticism of the present Pope, or any lawful successor to him, hardens and leads to militant action. This throws very great responsibility on critics. These may be theorists with no idea of a programme of action; they would possibly be surprised and shocked at the idea that their criticism would be so interpreted. The writer or public speaker is satisfied when he has given vent to his dissatisfaction, perhaps his antipathy or hatred. That fulfils his temperamental need, assuages his emotional enmity, leaves him with no further option. But the activist is not so psychologically structured. Ideas for him are not satisfying. He may be driven to do something; the impulse will vary with his personal resources, his sense of crisis, the opportunity given him for action. This opportunity depends on the support or collaboration he can expect from others. Thus revolutions - good and bad - have been, are being, made. The possibility of a revolution aimed at the very person of a reigning Pope depends on the number of people opposed to him, their readiness to take extreme measures, their calculation of the ultimate support that will be forthcoming. They might be ruthless, motivated, (consciously or subconsciously), by a perverse desire to change the direction the Church is taking. They may be persuaded, as are all revolutionaries, that they know best. With such conviction and such a drive they are not open to discussion. They are bent on results, which they think they can achieve, control and guarantee. How much they can do depends on how much the Spirit of God allows them to do within his own ultimate design. They may be his instruments of chastisement.

Apostasy

The Catholic Church was in a mood of euphoria as Vatican II came to an end, and
for some time afterwards. The Constitution on the Church in the Modern World, the
Decree on Ecumenism and the Declarations on the Relation of the Church to non-
Christian Religions and on Religious Liberty seemed to anticipate goodwill all round,
soon to be followed by disappearance of obstacles to growth in membership, ecclesial
expansion in quantitative and qualitative terms. The Church would win the modern
world to its side, it would come closer not only to other Christian bodies, but to the
adherents of the world religions; it could expect the trusting allegiance of true liberals
everywhere. Freed from an intellectual ghetto of rigid, dated formulas and a cast-
iron code of conduct, from ritual in a forgotten tongue, it would summon the best in
humankind and welcome a heartening response. Dialogue as an approach, pluralism
as a mental framework, lightening of the burden of history by disavowal or tardy
regret would combine to secure the triumph of a Church which resolutely renounced
triumphalism. We were on the threshold of a golden age. If we momentarily
debased the currency by bargaining over truth, truth divinely entrusted to us, by
thinning to the bone sacred doctrines and pieties, the stakes were high and the
recompense a certainty. Read in the terms of everyday, concrete realities the
expectation must be of more priests and religious, of alert wise spiritual rulers, of
a Church going forward enriched by charisms, manifesting in a new more captivating
way the especial mark of our fellowship, "See how these Christians love one
another."

Has it happened? What happened has been something totally different. It soon
became evident that there were immense problems within and outside the post-
conciliar Church. These probably surprised Paul VI; they certainly saddened him.
He spoke of the "auto-destruction" in the Church, and of the smoke of Satan which
had entered the Church "by a crack." To the French bishops he spoke sharply of the
aberrations in their country. These were documented by a brilliant Catholic writer,
Michel de St Pierre in two works, *Les fumées de Satan* and *Le ver est dans le fruit*;
he had, much earlier, shown the changes in clerical attitudes in *Les nouveaux prêtres*,
a documentary novel. One incident from real life woven into the fabric of that novel
was widely challenged as outlandish - priests doing a marxist retreat. The author
repeatedly stated that he had witnessed it!

Symptoms of the widespread religious decline were the identity crisis among priests
and religious, which led to many departures from the ministry and from the convents,
the drop in vocations, the non-practising masses, which merely grew in numbers.
Doctrinal dissent, noted in many places, came to a head in 1967 with the widespread
rejection of *Humanae Vitae*. Theological pluralism was wildly abused in places:
basic truths in theology, especially in Christology, Marian theology and Eucharistic
doctrine, were denied or deprived of their essential meaning. Only bad news is
news, so those with heretical or ambiguous opinions in the sacred sciences were

favoured and sheltered by the media.

All that would amount to something very serious. But it would be a religious void, not easily characterized as formal apostasy. This means rejection or repudiation of religious truth. Here the sects must be considered. Do all those who join them fully repudiate their Catholic faith? They are numerous and in 1992 the Pope summoned a special meeting of Cardinals to report on their impact worldwide. Figures are occasionally given, which may or may not be accurate: 3,000 in the United States and in Brazil; 350 in France. The latter figure is very surprising in view of the Catholic history of this country.

It is not necessary to enter into detail about the abandonment of Christian principles, of basic moral values - what Cardinal Ratzinger had in mind when he used the word "pagan" about certain areas. How has the Pope reacted? He has refused to compromise on truth. Without witch-hunts or repressive measures, he has continued to proclaim Christian and moral values challenged even by government legislation at the present time: the sanctity of marriage, the inalienable right to life from the first moment of existence. Not only in *Veritatis Splendor* and the Catechism of the Catholic Church, but on every occasion where it is necessary he is a fearless, articulate exponent of the imperatives of Christ's gospel. This he has done without pessimistic utterance.

The Pope has supported personal, enlightened witnesses to truth. He has retained beside him one of the great theologians of the age, Cardinal Ratzinger, as he honoured the outstanding theologian of the century, Hans Urs van Balthasar - among whose works, incidentally the reader may consult entitled, *The anti-Roman complex.* John Paul has likewise given every encouragement to the *International Catholic Commission*, a positively oriented body, which ensures proper presentation of Orthodox theology. He has recently founded the *Academy of Social Sciences* to ensure adequate diffusion of Catholic teaching in that world. Every medium of catechetics and evangelization has benefitted by his enlightened counsel and backing.

The Pope's travels, already to over sixty countries outside Italy - as to every important area within the country, are designed to give dignity and confidence to the local church wherever he goes. He sees that as Europe becomes a secularized wasteland, Africa, in the midst of political, economic and social difficulties is, with a vibrant Catholicism, providing a counter-weight to the old continent. Hence he has by now, in eleven journeys, practically covered the continent.

The distinguished French journalist, André Frossard, convert son of a former general secretary of the communist party, points to John Paul's defence of human rights. The fall of the communist regimes, and the opening towards the world religions, especially the Jews (see articles *Assisi* and *Jews, The*), enhance the credibility of the Pope's teaching. His innovative apostolate of youth (qv) does likewise.

Shining through all his apostolate, pastoral activity and teaching is the sheer indisputable holiness of the man himself. "Men learn at the school of example as at no other" said Edmund Burke. Here certainly is Christian example in excelsis. A crushing work-load from early morning till late at night, despite health problems; a serene, unshaken approach to every vicissitude that this distracted age may cause or occasion.

Yet, people may ask, what results are there to show? A saintly Pope cannot deprive people of their freedom, to abuse which they may have been manipulated, indoctrinated, or misled in so many different ways; multiple pressures towards evil-doing exist at the present time. But anyone with knowledge of the true faithful knows one thing: the more wickedness increases, the more opposition to the Pope hardens, the more fervent souls grow in fidelity, devotion, constant prayer for the successor of Peter. The call is for heroism and it is being answered in Christian terms.

Nor is the future irretrievably dark. The reader is referred to the article on the Orthodox (see also *Catechism of the Catholic Church* and *Veritatis Splendor*, especially *Spirit, The Holy*).

Apparitions of Our Lady

Pope John Paul is through and through Marian (see *Mary, Mother of God*). He must then be sensitive to experience of Our Lady in the Church at the present time. Particularly conspicuous in this experience in recent decades are apparitions of Our Lady. We live in the century most favoured by Marian apparitions and the number has increased recently most remarkably. A very conservative estimate for the whole century is three hundred. A list is appended to this article of those which occurred or were given prominence, either by being declared authentic or by stirring an important movement of piety during the pontificate of John Paul II. It is a worldwide phenomenon, one effect of which has been to encourage those who held on to Marian devotion during the dark years that followed the Council, what the biblical scholar, Ignace de la Potterie SJ called at the International Mariological Congress in Huelva, in September, 1952, "a decade without Mary."

John Paul II has shown in *Christifideles Laici* that he values charisms. Between him and those favoured by apparitions of Our Lady, the Spirit is the bond (see *Spirit, The Holy*). He is guided by the Holy Spirit in his Petrine service to the body of Christ which is his Church; they are recipients of special graces given by the Spirit as he wills: given for the good of the body.

The story of visionaries is a disgraceful one in the Catholic Church. They have been at times persecuted by members of the clergy, treated almost as enemies of the Church; the generalization is not lightly made; it rests on research. Prudence is generally invoked as the supreme need. Prudence is needed throughout the whole of life. Discernment is required in dealing with apparitions; the criteria have been explained by a Roman document issued not so long ago. The best known apparitions occurring during the Pope's pontificate have been at Medjugorje. Here there was a calamitous error in teaching by the local hierarchy. On 27/28 November, 1991 the bishops issued a statement asserting that they could not say that the apparitions and revelations were supernatural in origin. This was their response to the most detailed examination ever made of such phenomena. Every relevant discipline was represented in this examination: mystical theology, history, medicine, psychology, neurology. Experts were on hand in every sector; every informed judgement was favourable.

So were two tests of still wider significance, the *sensus fidelium* and the Master's word, "Judge the tree by its fruits." The *sensus fidelium* or deep-seated conviction of the faithful Christian people is exemplified in the ten million (very conservative estimate) pilgrims who have flocked to Medjugorje from all over the world, in the scores of thousands of prayer groups originating in faith sprung from Medjugorje (six thousand in three Australian cities, Melbourne, Sydney, Brisbane), in the numerous periodical publications reporting what happens, in the presence over the years of 20,000 priests and one hundred bishops.

And the fruits? How many conversions have taken place? Five hundred and seventy miracles have been recorded. The revival of sacramental life is shown in the huge number of confessions: over one hundred and fifty confessors have been needed at times; this happens nowhere else in the Catholic Church in our time. Let us not overlook the extraordinary signs, the appearances of the Virgin, the miracles of the sun, the mysterious images seen in the heavens; so much else.

Apparitions reported elsewhere: San Nicolas, Argentine, 1983; Cuenca, Ecuador, 1988; Scottsdale, Arizona, 1988; Betania, Venezuela, 1976, approved 1987; Cuapa, Nicaragua, 1980; Mount Melleray, Ireland, 1984; Naju, South Korea, 1985; Akita, Japan, 1973, approved 1981; Mayfield, Ireland, 1988; Kibeho, Africa, 1981; Souphanieh, Syria, 1986.

The Pope's reaction? He told Bishop Hlnilica that if he were not Pope he would have long ago gone to Medjugorje. He advised a Brazilian bishop to go there; he told Bishop Kim, president of the Korean episcopal committee, that what had taken place in Eastern Europe was due to Our Lady, as she had stated at Fatima and Medjugorje.

Dealing with current literature *Catechesi Tradendae* is quite realistic. A quotation
is appropriate:

> Among these various ways and means - all the Church's activities have a
> catechetical dimension - catechetical works, far from losing their essential
> importance, acquire fresh significance. One of the major features of the renewal
> of catechetics today is the rewriting and multiplication of catechetical books
> taking place in many parts of the Church. Numerous very successful works have
> been produced and are a real treasure in the service of catechetical instruction.
> But it must be humbly and honestly recognized that this rich flowering has
> brought with it articles and publications which are ambiguous and harmful to
> young people and to the life of the Church. In certain places, the desire to find
> the best forms of expression or to keep up with fashions in pedagogical methods
> has often enough resulted in certain catechetical works which bewilder the young
> and even adults, either by deliberately or unconsciously omitting elements
> essential to the Church's faith, or by attributing excessive importance to certain
> themes at the expense of others, or chiefly, by a rather horizontalist overall view
> out of keeping with the teaching of the Church's Magisterium.

> Therefore, it is not enough to multiply catechetical works. In order that these
> works may correspond with their aim, several conditions are essential:

> a.   They must be linked with the real life of the generation to which they are
>   addressed, showing close acquaintance with its anxieties and questionings,
>   struggles and hopes.
> b.   They must try to speak a language comprehensible to the generation in
>   question.
> c.   They must make a point of giving the whole message of Christ and his
>   Church, without neglecting or distorting anything, and in expounding it they
>   will follow a line and structure that highlights what is essential.
> d.   They must really aim to give to those who use them a better knowledge of
>   the mysteries of Christ, aimed at true conversion and a life more in
>   conformity with God's will.

These strictures and suggestions must be seen in the overall teaching of the Apostolic
Exhortation, which is positive, optimistic, Christ-centric. True to the general thesis
of the present summary of John Paul II's teaching attention is drawn to the
concluding section of the Holy Spirit:

> At the end of this Apostolic Exhortation, the gaze of my heart turns to him who is the
> principle, inspiring all catechetical work and all who do this work - the Spirit of the
> Father and of the Son, the Holy Spirit. In describing the mission that this Spirit would
> have in the Church, Christ used the significant words: 'He will teach you all things,
> and bring to your remembrance all that I have said to you' (Jn 14:26).

And he added:

> 'When the Spirit of truth comes, he will guide you into all the truth..he will declare to you all the things that are to come' (Jn 16:13).

The Spirit thus promised to the Church and to each Christian as a Teacher within, who, in the secret of the conscience and the heart, makes one understand what one has heard but was not capable of grasping: 'Even now the Holy Spirit teaches the faithful' said St Augustine in this regard, 'in accordance with each one's spiritual capacity. And he sets their hearts aflame with greater desire according as each one progresses in the charity that makes him love what he already knows and desire what he has yet to know.'

Furthermore, the Spirit's mission is also to transform the disciples into witnesses to Christ: 'He will bear witness to me; and you are also his witnesses.' (Jn 15:26-27)

But this is not all. For Saint Paul, who on this matter synthesizes a theology that is latent throughout the New Testament, it is the whole of one's 'being a Christian', the whole of the Christian life, the new life of the children of God, that constitutes a life in accordance with the Spirit (cf. Rom 8:14-17; Gal 4:6). Only the Spirit enables us to say to God, 'Abba, Father' (Rom 8:15). Without the Spirit we cannot say: 'Jesus is Lord' (1 Cor 12:3). From the Spirit come all the charisms that build up the Church, the community of Christians (cf. 1 Cor 12:4-11). In keeping with this, Saint Paul gives each disciple of Christ the instruction: 'Be filled with the Spirit' (Eph 5:18). Saint Augustine is very explicit: 'Both (our believing and our doing good) are ours because of the choice of our will, and yet both are gifts from the Spirit of faith and charity.'

Catechesis, which is growth in faith and the maturing of Christian life towards its fullness, is consequently a work of the Holy Spirit, a work that he alone can initiate and sustain in the Church.

This realization, based on the text quoted above and on many other passages of the New Testament, convinces us of two things.

To begin with, it is clear that, when carrying out her mission of giving catechesis, the Church - and also every individual Christian devoting himself to that mission within the Church and in her name - must be very much aware of acting as a living pliant instrument of the Holy Spirit. To invoke this Spirit constantly, to be in communion with him, to endeavour to know his authentic inspirations must be the attitude of the teaching Church and of every catechist.

Secondly, the deep desire to understand better the Spirit's action and to entrust oneself to him more fully - at a time when 'in the Church we are living an exceptionally favourable season of the Spirit' as my predecessor Paul VI remarked in his Apostolic Exhortation *Evangelii Nuntiandi* - must bring about a catechetical awakening. For 'renewal in the Spirit' will be authentic and will have real fruitfulness in the Church, not so much according as it gives rise to extraordinary charisms, but according as it leads the greatest possible number of the faithful as they travel their daily paths, to make a humble, patient and persevering effort to know the mystery of Christ better and better, and to bear witness to it. I invoke on the catechizing Church this Spirit of the Father and the Son, and I beg him to renew catechetical dynamism in the Church.

The Pope ends, as he does all his important texts with a consideration on Mary (qv). It begins thus: "May the Virgin of Pentecost obtain this for us through her intercession..."

Catechism of the Catholic Church, The

A catechism or compendium of the faith was issued after the Council of Trent, *Catechismus ex Decreto Concilii Tridenti ad Parochos*. It has been a basic text over the intervening period. Many catechisms have been published adapted to local needs or to problems of the particular age. After Vatican II the Dutch bishops issued a summary of the Catholic faith which was widely noted; some points were corrected in a review made in Rome and notice was given to the faithful. Recently the hierarchies of France and of Germany published catechisms suited to adults; the German text was submitted to Rome before being distributed. Each is excellent.

The present Catechism is John Paul's response to a request made for such a compendium by the members of the Extraordinary Synod called in 1985 by the Pope for the twentieth anniversary of Vatican II. The next year he set up a commission of twelve Cardinals and Bishops, with Cardinal Ratzinger as president to work out an agenda, and a drafting committee of seven diocesan Bishops to collaborate in the work. The Austrian Dominican, Christoph von Schönborn, was named secretary general.

In his presentation of the final text the Pope could say that in the drafting of nine successive versions, there had been consultation "of all the Catholic bishops, of their episcopal conferences and synods, of institutes of theology and catechesis." In the *Motu Proprio, Ecclesia Dei Afflicta* published some days after the excommunication of Mgr Marcel Lefebvre (qv) he stated:

The breadth and profoundity of Vatican II teachings necessitate a fresh and thorough reflection, in order to highlight the Council's continuity with Tradition, particularly on those points of doctrine which, perhaps because of their novelty, have not been completely understood in certain sectors of the Church.

The Pope, in his introduction to the Catechism enlightens the reader on its general plan and purpose:

> A catechism ought to present faithfully and in organic form the teaching of Sacred Scripture, of the living Tradition in the Church and of the authentic Magisterium, as well as the spiritual legacy of the Fathers, of men and women saints of the Church, to allow the Christian mystery to be better known, and to revive the faith of the People of God. It must take account of the instances when doctrine has been explained as the Holy Spirit suggested to the Church in the passage of time. It must also help to clarify in the light of faith new situations, and problems not posed in the past.
>
> The Catechism will then include what is new and what is old (cf Mt 13:52), the faith being always the same, and the source of lights ever new.
>
> To meet this double demand the Catechism of the Catholic Church, on the one hand adopts the 'ancient' traditional order, already followed by the Catechism of Pius V, dividing its contents in four parts: the Credo; the holy liturgy, with the sacraments in priority; Christian action, on the basis of the commandments; and finally Christian prayer. But at the same time, the contents are often expressed in a 'new' manner, the better to answer questionings of our time.
>
> The four parts are linked with each other: the Christian mystery is the object of faith (part one); it is celebrated and communicated in liturgical actions (part two); it is present to enlighten and support the children of God in their action (part three); it is the basis of our prayer, of which the Our Father is the privileged expression, and it constitutes the object of our request, our praise and our intercession (part four).
>
> The liturgy is itself prayer; the confession of faith has its right place in the celebration of cult. Grace, fruit of the Sacraments, is the irreplaceable condition of Christian action, just as participation in the Church's liturgy demands faith. If faith does not produce works it remains dead (Js 2:14-26).
>
> Reading the Catechism of the Catholic Church one can grasp the admirable unity of the mystery of God, of his plan for salvation, and the central place of Jesus Christ, only Son of God, sent by the Father, become man in the womb of the most Holy Virgin Mary by the Holy Spirit to be our Saviour. Dead and risen he is always present in the Church, especially in the Sacraments; He is the source of faith, the model of Christian action, and the Master of our prayer.

A prologue by the editors gives further help to understand the plan of the work and to use it profitably. There is ample flexibility in the distribution of themes. Every thematic unity is followed by a succinct summary to facilitate understanding and memory. Important authors from the early centuries to modern times figure in the sources; so do all important prouncements from the Magisterium, conciliar or papal. In this respect the riches command admiration.

Technically the French edition, which we must use since the English version is not yet available, is very well edited, as to lay-out, variation in type-face, annotation which is plenary without being oppressive, indexing, varied and exhaustive.

It is not surprising that the book has had a wide appeal; within a few months it sold a million copies in French-speaking countries. It answers a need felt by many people: clear affirmation of religious truth with adequate motivation.

Cracow

One of the great cities and cultural centres of Eastern Europe, Cracow has an ancient university, second in antiquity only to that in Prague. It was the royal city, is dominated by the Wawel, pantheon of the kings of Poland. It did not suffer the physical assault made on Warsaw as the occupying forces withdrew (Frank to Hitler, "We are leaving Warsaw, but so that no Pole will ever again live in it"). In the time of Karol Wojtyla the diocese had a population of about a million and a half with over 1,500 priests, secular and religious, about the same number of religious brothers and as many nuns. (See article *Faustina Kowalska, Blessed*)

In 1948 Fr Karol Wojtyla returned to work in his native country. The regime would see to it that he had little scope for social work of the kind that he had studied in the French and Belgian Young Christian movement. Cardinal Sapieha (qv) at first seemed to provide little scope for his intellectual progress, although he seemed destined for the academic world, his scholarly attainments being of the highest. His first appointment was to a country curacy in the village of Niegowice, near Wieliczka. Soon afterwards he was changed to a city parish in Cracow, St Florian's. In both assignments he was esteemed for his interest in people, his modest even impoverished life-style, his easy manner, his readiness when visiting parishioners around Christmas time to join in carol singing. His habits of prayer, his hours in the chapel before the Blessed Sacrament, his whole bearing as a priest and his fidelity to duty were, for people in need of spiritual support, the things that really counted.

While engaged in pastoral ministry in St Florian's, Fr Wojtyla returned to university studies at Cracow University. Under the direction of Fr Wladyslaw Wicher, he prepared for his doctorate in theology, specialising in moral theology. That was but a preliminary to his real ambition, which was to devote a dissertation to a problem which fascinated him: the possibility of reconciling modern philosophy with the Thomism he had studied in Rome.   One is reminded of the pioneering work accomplished by Cardinal Mercier in Louvain University.   To qualify for the degree of Agrégé of Cracow University Karol Wojtyla prepared a dissertation on the possibility of founding a Christian ethic on the system of Max Scheler.   The dissertation was defended in 1953.   It appeared in print from the Press of the University of Lublin in 1959.

In time Cracow meant a diocese, to help govern which he was named Auxiliary Bishop in 1958, which he would rule as Archbishop from 1963, with the title of Cardinal from 1967.   As seventy-sixth Ordinary of the ancient royal capital of Poland, he was the first commoner in the long line.   He had no complex about his proletarian background, nor reluctance to admit it.   He had invited to his episcopal ordination the workers of the Solway factory who had been kind to him when he worked with them.   The faithful of the diocese would in time learn that humble origins are no bar to religious and cultural distinction.

Pope John-Paul II would speak warmly of the special relationship which grew up between Bishop and people:

> Old and new Cracow, the new districts, the new people, the new suburbs, Nowa Huta; concern for the urgency of new churches and new parishes; the new needs of evangelisation, catechesis and the apostolate.   All this accompanies me on St Peter's Chair.   All this constitutes a layer of my soul which I cannot leave.   The layer of my experience, of my faith of my love which expands to embrace so many places dear to me, so many sanctuaries of Christ and his Mother, such as Mogila, Ludmierz, Myslenic Staniatki or Rychwald and particularly Kalvaria Zebrzydowka with its paths along which I walked with such pleasure.   I keep in my eyes and in my heart the panorama of the land of Cracow, Zywiec, Slask Podhale, Beskidy and Tatra.   I offer to the Lord this beloved land and the whole landscape of Poland, but especially its people.

Kalvaria Zebrzydowda is a reproduction over a whole stretch of rolling countryside near Cracow of the Way of the Cross.   The future Pope often went there to pray.

His time as Archbishop was consumed with multiple activities.   He was obliged to leave the modest apartment where he had been approachable to all, especially students, and take up residence in the official abode of the Archbishop.   Here he quickly found a means of thwarting the government's ban on Catholic associations. Responsible for the Lay Apostolate he took to inviting different groups to spend an evening with him, share an oplatek wafer, take a little wine and then engage in the earnest, lively conversation that the Poles love: the subject, whatever happened to affect their lifework or interests directly.   Their host could communicate with them in their own idiom.

Intellectual matters were a high priority. After the total destruction of the Polish intelligentsia (see *Second World War*) a renaissance had taken place. The Archbishop of Cracow was active in this recovery of an agelong heritage - this is a people with prodigious potential in whatever touches the human mind. He was available for scholarly lectures at congresses at home and abroad; he sponsored or supported important conventions of a philosophical or theological kind. In another domain akin to this, journalism, he was in constant contact with Jerzy Turowicz, editor of *Tygodnik Powszechny*, the most respected Catholic journalist in eastern Europe. The editor could count on him for contributions, not necessarily signed; eventually the paper would also print poems by the Archbishop.

Nor was pastoral care in any way neglected; all that has been mentioned was also seen in a pastoral perspective. More evidently so, the preparation of the diocesan synod due to assemble in 1979 was widespread and thorough. The Archbishop also collaborated wholeheartedly with the preparations for the Polish Millennium, a nine year programme leading up to 1966. And he was available as a Polish representative at the two important synods in Rome, 1971 on the priesthood and 1974 on evangelization. In the course of the first he addressed a press conference on an exemplary priest, his fellow countryman, Maximilian Kolbe, who was beatified at the time, 17 October. In the second he had the duty of preparing the report on the theological aspect of the problem. This was one of the principal documents of the synod submitted to Paul VI. It is thought that its content so impressed the Pope that he was thereby led to invite the author to preach the papal retreat in 1976.

Critics

There are three preliminaries to criticism of a Pope. A Pope must follow his conscience, and in this age when conscience is so highly valued, it is important to stress that it is the Pope's conscience, not that of his critics, which counts. Secondly, the Pope has advisory bodies, sources of information, not available to his critics. Thirdly, in matters of great seriousness, the Pope must rely on the direct action of the Holy Spirit. Now there is no theological guarantee that the Holy Spirit informs his critics on the content of the inspiration of the Pope, on his precise impulse, and on the degree of fidelity which he meets.

But there are matters of public policy which involve the whole Church, where the Pope may be just the spokesman, the interpreter of an ecclesial thrust, either in doctrine or devotion: such would probably be the response of those who criticize Popes. Evidently certain decisions are more strictly within the Pope's competence, and his alone, or the normal mechanism of papal information may not function. Before dismissing Cardinal Mindszenty - tragically but a few months before his death - Pope Paul VI believed that all the Hungarian bishops wished this done. He was, it is now known, misinformed.

It is one of the remarkable strengths of John Paul II that he can withstand criticism equably, with no bitterness, no retaliation, no flinching on the line of duty. His critics will have the unenviable place in history of evoking this truly Christian response. They differ in outlook and background, from the extreme right, represented by the *Catholic Counter-Reformation of the Twentieth Century* led by Abbé Georges de Nantes to progressive theologians and journalists, or media performers generally.

Critics sometimes point to episcopal appointments which have roused local protest, for example in Chur (Switzerland) and in Dutch, German or Brazilian dioceses, as signs of John Paul's preference for conservatives. People tend to take an insular view of episcopal appointments in general, thinking that it is unforgivable to name a bishop who does not belong to the local diocesan clergy. A little history would show that bishops have been chosen in very different ways through the ages. One of the greatest was the result of popular acclamation, the subject not even being baptised, Ambrose of Milan, a catechumen, effective imperial ruler of all northern Italy. The See of Milan has very often had someone from outside its boundaries to rule it; so has Paris and so has Westminster, to mention but a few. In fact for centuries the European monarchs named the bishops in their realms. In certain areas a local priest will be unpopular as bishop; an outsider is preferred.

The onus to appoint bishops is put on the Pope in recent church legislation. It is understandable that John Paul II would choose men of personal integrity, sound in doctrine, loyal to the Church and to the Papacy. The vast majority of his nominees are irreproachable. But appointing bishops is not the substantive element of his mission. This is teaching, evangelization, ecumenism, opening to the world as it is, understanding of the great world religions (see articles, *Mission, Youth, Assisi* and those on doctrinal subjects, *Ecumenism, Orthodox, Jews* etc...) Ideas forward humankind to its destiny and this man has already given a rich harvest of ideas, stamped with his distinctive philosophic outlook, rooted in both Thomism and phenomenology, welcoming valid biblical insights, sensitive to the deep currents of human reflection and striving.

Again his critics regret his support of Opus Dei (qv). They forget that when the first bishop-prelate, Mgr Alvaro del Portillo died suddenly on 23 March, 1993, this organisation had 80,000 members, 1,500 priests (700 in the last nine years), existed in eighty countries. What Pope could refuse support to such a vigorous body? Is there any other order or congregation which has ordained 700 priests in the last nine, often barren, years? John Paul honoured the deceased superior as if he were a Cardinal, praised him highly.

He supports *Communione e Liberazione*! Thank God he does. A society with such

in the section entitled "The Spirit and the Bride say 'Come.'" In the conclusion the Trinitarian idea which recurs is made explicit:

> He is the Spirit of the Father and of the Son; like the Father and the Son he is uncreated, without limit, eternal, omnipotent, God, Lord (creed *Quicunque, DS 75*)... Before him I kneel at the end of these considerations, and implore him, as the Spirit of the Father and the Son, to grant to all of us the *blessing and grace*, which I desire to pass on, in the name of the Most Holy Trinity, to the sons and daughters of the Church and to the whole human family (67).

The Encyclical is a worthy contribution from the Teaching Authority to the varied literature on the Holy Spirit in our age.

Ecumenism

In regard to ecumenism the pontificate of John Paul II must be examined from these aspects: teaching and legislation which he has supervised and stamped with his authority; example in practice. His teaching is admirably contained in the *Catechism of the Catholic Church*, which faithfully expounds what was laid down in the *Decree on Ecumenism* by Vatican II - there are over forty references to the Decree in the course of the text. In occasional addresses to personalities or representative groups from the other Christian churches one finds ideas which reflect the Pope's teaching, the development of his thought.

Legislation is framed in the Code of Canon Law (qv) which he officially promulgated in 1983. Thus Canon 755 states that it belongs to the entire episcopal college and to the Apostolic See "to promote and direct the participation of Catholics in the ecumenical movement." The reason given is that the unity of all is the "will of Christ." Bishops too are to work for ecumenism in their jurisdiction seeing to "practical norms." Canon 383.3 dictates the behaviour of the individual bishop: "He is to act with kindness and charity toward those who are not in full communion with the Catholic Church, fostering ecumenism as it is understood by the Church." Canon 844 is most important, as it deals with the Sacraments. Catholics may, if so situated that they have no access to Sacraments in their own Church, receive them from ministers of other Churches which have valid Sacraments.

The vital words are those dealing with non-Catholics seeking the Sacraments in Catholic Churches:

> Catholic ministers may licitly administer the Sacraments of Penance, Eucharist and Anointing of the sick to members of the Oriental churches which do not have full communion with the Catholic Church, if they ask on their own for the Sacraments and are properly disposed.

More guarded is the following directive:

> This holds too for members of other churches which, in the judgement of the
> Apostolic See, are in the same condition as the Oriental Churches as far as these
> Sacraments are concerned.

An ecumenical Directory was issued in two parts, in 1967 and 1970. The passage
of time, and the experience acquired thereby, showed that it needed revision and
enlargement. Speaking to the plenary session of the Secretariat for Christian Unity
in 1988 the Pope noted that:

> the breadth of the ecumenical movement, the multiplication of dialogue
> statements, the urgent need that is felt for a greater participation by the whole
> People of God in this movement, and the consequent necessity of accurate
> doctrinal information, in view of a proper commitment, all of this requires that
> up-to-date directives be given without delay.

The result of the labours expended on this work is a text which is much more than
twice the size of the first Directory, and very comprehensive in its contents.
Everything is dealt with and composition is appropriate. The Pope gave his approval
on 25 March, 1993.

What example has he given in the practice of ecumenism? In his first Encyclical,
Redemptor Hominis, he emphasized the importance of the cause of Christian unity,
recalling with gratitude what John XXIII and Paul VI had done. He knew that some
were discouraged at what they thought meagre results, would wish to turn back. His
own determination was thus expressed:

> It is also certain that in the present historical situation of Christianity and the
> world the only possibility we see of fulfilling the Church's universal mission,
> with regard to ecumenical questions is that of seeking sincerely, perseveringly,
> humbly and also courageously the ways of drawing closer and of union. Pope
> Paul VI gave us his personal example for this.

> We must therefore seek unity without being discouraged at the difficulties that
> can appear or accumulate along that road, otherwise we would be unfaithful to
> the word of Christ, we would fail to accomplish his testament. Have we the
> right to run this risk? (n.6)

Over the years John Paul II has not missed an opportunity to implement this
programme. Some examples of his action will suffice. On 29 May, 1982, with
Archbishop Runcie of Canterbury, in the Cathedral church, he signed a declaration
which looked back to the meeting of Paul VI and Archbishop Michael Ramsey, to

ARCIC and its achievement, and ended with these words:

> Confident in the power of this same Holy Spirit, we commit ourselves anew to the task of working for unity with firm faith, renewed hope and ever deeper love.

He spoke words of similar confidence and resolve on 12 June, 1984 at the World Council of Churches. He did advise Archbishop Carie that the ordination of women would create a major obstacle to unity.

The seventh assembly of the World Council of Churches took place in Canberra from 7-20 February, 1991, on a theme dear to the Pope: "Come Holy Spirit - Renew the Whole Creation." He sent a written message, which contained these words:

> The ecumenical movement, of which your assembly is an important forum has been 'fostered by the grace of the Holy Spirit.' ...My visit to the World Council of Churches in 1984 and your subsequent visit to Rome underlined the significant efforts towards unity in which we are engaged... May your assembly be an occasion of a renewed awareness of the Spirit's gifts in this regard. (*Signs of the Spirit - Official Report*, Seventh Assembly, Geneva, 1991, Decree on Ecumenism p.269-270).

The Pope is especially devoted to union with the Orthodox. A Catholic delegation regularly goes to Istanbul to join in the celebration of St Andrew's feast day. A message from John Paul II to the Patriarch accompanies them. On 28 June 1992 Meliton of Chalcedoine was in Rome as delegate of the Patriarch with admirable exchange of messages. On 31 May, 1991 the Pope sent a special letter to European bishops on the relations between Catholics and Orthodox in central and eastern Europe with the changed political situation. On 5 June of that year he visited the Orthodox church in Bialystok, in his native country: he used such words as "beloved brothers and sisters in Christ", evoked "the deep sacramental roots of this fraternity." Influenced possibly by the writings of Vassula Rydén (qv) John Paul has appealed to the Orthodox to unite the feast of Easter. In the Stations of the Cross, on Good Friday, 1994, he was followed by an Orthodox prelate.

Education

In 1931, Karol Wojtyla, his primary schooling finished, entered the Wadowice secondary school. Have we reliable information on his student achievement? Has the amazing subsequent career thrown back over the early years a glow of artificial light and triumph? The anti-triumphalists have some obstacles, some certain facts. In Karol's last year, 1939, Archbishop Adam Stefan Sapieha (qv) of Cracow (qv) came on a visit to the school. Schools were not then a bone of contention between

Church and State, and Fr Edward Zacher, teacher of religious knowledge, was a member of the staff. The address of welcome to the Archbishop was read by Karol Wojtyla. Sapieha asked Fr Zacher did this boy, who impressed him, have any idea of the priesthood. The answer was negative.

The report sheet on the boy's final year at the school would also have impressed Sapieha. It shows that for conduct and six subjects - religious knowledge, Polish, Latin, Greek, German, Mathematics - his note was "very good", the highest, and for three subjects - physics, chemistry he got "good." Fr Zacher, who taught him for six years, said at the time of the papal election, that he was the nearest thing to a schoolboy genius he ever met. Another teacher, Helena Szcepanska, said that Karol was the best in the school in Greek and Latin: "He sometimes embarrassed us; he seemed to know more than we did."

When Karol's secondary studies were complete, the family moved to Cracow. One of its glories is the Jagiellonian University, an institution prominent in the life of the future Pope. The elder brother was to pursue medical studies and enter the profession. He would die young, a victim of scarlatina. Karol enrolled as a student of Polish language and literature, and philosophy. For a career his thoughts turned principally to the stage. He joined Studio Dramatyczne, a student group which put on plays of Polish historical interest, as well as modern works. Karol's performance in one play, "Moonlight Cavalier", by Marian Nijinski, was enthusiastically recalled by his fellow actors and actresses. The play was a hit, was well publicised and reviewed, and was for long referred to in histories of the Cracow theatre.

In the choice of companions and recreation Karol's emphasis was very much on culture. He met with friends for verse readings, their own compositions or poetry published by authors whom they liked. His choice was often the work of Emil Zegadlowicz, like himself a native of Wadowice. One of these ardent young people Mieczyslaw Kotlarczyk, was to reach fame in the Polish theatre. A book dealing with his attainments as an actor entitled *The Art of the Living Word*, carries a preface by his lifelong friend, by this time Archbishop of Cracow.

In September 1939 the world crashed about the two young friends. The ancient enemies of Poland had made an evil pact. The Poles did not provoke Hitler's paranoiac temper, his ruthless anti-semitism as did the Jews. They stung him, none the less, to a sustained icy fury. They refused to surrender. Alone of all his victims they gave him no quisling; their defiance was total; their honour resplendent.

Wojtyla felt the evil in his very vocational aspiration. The University of Cracow was closed. On 6 November, 1939 the entire teaching staff was assembled and, to their surprise and horror, taken off to concentration camps. Many of these teachers were world famous scholars. Seventeen of them died in detention; the others, as a result of world protest and pressure, were eventually released.

in Coimbra. He pronounced a lengthy prayer to the Immaculate Heart of Mary, on the occasion of his first visit.

Previous Popes have been identified with Fatima. Pius XII adverted to the fact that his episcopal ordination took place on 13 May, 1917 - he was going to Bavaria as Nuncio. On 31 October 1942, in the course of a broadcast to Fatima closing the Silver Jubilee celebrations, he consecrated the world to the Immaculate Heart of Mary. In a broadcast on 13 May, 1946 he outlined a theology of the Queenship of Mary, which he would proclaim on 1 November, 1954, issuing at the same time his Encyclical *Ad Caeli Reginam*. On 13 May, 1967 Paul VI (qv) went to Fatima for the Golden Jubilee, despite criticism arising in the period of scepticism about Our Lady which followed Vatican II. Some of his critics yielded before overwhelming popular acclaim. The Pope published at the time his first important text on Our Lady for the Golden Jubilee of the apparitions, *Signum Magnum*; it would be followed by the masterly *Marialis Cultus* in 1974. In Fatima the Pope was publicly seen at the shrine with Sister Lucia.

Fatima, The Secret of

The Pope knows the third secret of Fatima. Like his immediate predecessors, John XXIII and Paul VI, he has not divulged it. Can we guess its contents? Some suggestions are here mentioned, with reservation. In November 1980, John Paul II was in Fulda and was asked while talking to a small group of German Catholics what had become of the secret; was it not to be revealed in 1960? What would happen to the Church. His reply was given in *Stimme des Glaubens*:

> Because of the seriousness of its contents, in order not to encourage the world-wide power of Communism to carry out certain coups, my predecessors in the Chair of Peter have diplomatically preferred to withhold its publication.

> On the other hand it should be sufficient for all Christians to know this much: if there is a message in which it is said that the oceans will flood entire sections of the earth; that, from one moment to the other, millions of people will perish...there is no longer any point in really wanting to publish this secret message.

> Many want to know more out of curiosity, or because of their taste for sensationalism, but they forget that 'to know' implies for them responsibility. It is dangerous to want to satisfy one's curiosity only, if one is convinced that we can do nothing against a catastrophe that has been predicted.

"Here" said the Pope, holding his Rosary "is the remedy against all evil. Pray, pray and ask for nothing else. Put everything in the hands of the Mother of God." The Pope continued:

> We must be prepared to undergo great trials in the not too distant future; trials that will require us to be ready to give up even our lives, and a total gift of self to Christ and for Christ. Through your prayers and mine, it is possible to alleviate this tribulation, but it is no longer possible to avert it, because it is only in this way that the Church can be effectively renewed. How many times indeed, has the renewal of the Church been effected in blood? This time, again, it will not be otherwise.

> We must be strong, we must prepare ourselves, we must entrust ourselves to Christ and to his Holy Mother, and we must be attentive, very attentive to the prayer of the Rosary."

Cardinal Ratzinger has read the secret. He was asked by a friend, (whose name is withheld) what were its contents: "Akita" was his reply. This is possibly a reference to a prediction in a message given by Our Lady to Sister Agnes Sasagawa; the apparitions or revelations of Akita have been approved:

> If men do not repent and amend their lives, the Father is going to inflict a terrible chastisement on all of mankind. It will be a chastisement more serious than the deluge, such as no one has ever yet seen. A fire will fall from heaven and will annihilate a great part of humanity... The only arms which will remain to you will be the Rosary and the sign which the Son has left. Pray the Rosary every day for the Pope, the bishops, the priests. The action of the devil will infiltrate even into the Church. There will be many in the Church who will accept compromises. The demon will press many priests and consecrated souls to leave the service of the Lord. He will rage especially against souls consecrated to God. The thought of the loss of human souls (not lives) makes me sad. Already the cup overflows... I have prevented the coming of calamities by offering to the Father together with all the victim souls who console him, the sufferings endured by the Son on the Cross, by His blood and by His very loving soul. Prayer, penance and courageous sacrifices can appease the anger of the Father.

Some years back the Italian writer Don Luigi Bianchi published a book entitled *Fatima aveva ragione: Profezia e realtà del secolo* (Como 1992). Therein he hazarded the opinion that the "secret" of Fatima was the recent, continuing apostasy. A Vatican prelate who knew the secret read his book. To the question, "would you change anything?" his answer was "no."

There have been, in statements attributed to Sister Lucia, predictions of "Cardinal against Cardinal, bishop against bishop." This would be one element in the confusion, which for some is already more than incipient. Have we been spared the worst? Impossible to say.

Faustina Kowalska, Blessed (d. 1938)

This saintly person is widely known as the apostle of Divine Mercy. Her Diary is an indispensable source book for those seeking to understand her role and the underlying doctrine of her mission. Though born in the Province of Lodz and having spent much time in Vilinius she came, at the end of her short life, to Cracow; she was a perpetually professed member of the Congregation of Sisters of Our Lady of Mercy. She died 5 October, 1938. On 21 October, 1965 Archbishop Karol Wojtyla's delegate, Bishop Julian Groblicki, initiated solemnly the Informative Process preliminary to her Beatification. The Process was solemnly closed on 20 September, 1967 by Cardinal Wojtyla. Pope John Paul II beatified Faustina on 18 April 1993. It is a reasonable conjecture that the Pope was influenced in the choice of subject for his second Encyclical (qv), *Dives in Misericordia*, on Divine Mercy, by study of Blessed Faustina's message.

Are those right who believe that she predicted the election of a Polish Pope? The relevant words in her Diary are:

> As I was praying for Poland, I heard the words: I bear a special love for Poland, and if she will be obedient to my will, I will exalt her in might and holiness. From her will come forth the spark that will prepare the world for my final coming. (Notebook VI, 1732, ed. Stockbridge, Mass., 1987)

Finances of the Vatican

"For many years the financial structure of the Vatican was a secret even to the Pope himself. Within the Curia there were autonomous financial corporations, power centres that were reluctant to accept control." Thus a commentator highly qualified explains the situation which confronted Paul VI when he became Pope. True, much good was being done, but clouds had descended on the agencies handling and managing Vatican monies, as financial scandals had rocked Italy. There is no question of imputing blame to named individuals: those who died tragically kept many secrets, Michele Sindona and Roberto Calvi. Paul VI in 1967, with the Apostolic Constitution *Regimini Ecclesiae Apostolicae* aimed at a thorough reform of the central church administration, the Roman Curia. To effect the changes he deemed necessary in the financial agencies took time and patience. Vested interests inside the Curia slowed the process of reform. As late as 1991 it was clear that the financial agencies of the Vatican, in particular the *Institute for Religious Works*, could be used for shady dealings. A court case revealed that this organ, the "Pope's Bank" had been exploited; it had been used to channel some fifty million dollars in bribes to Italian politicians.

John Paul II acted to put an end to any such potential scandals. He accepted the affirmation of Paul VI, "The Church must be poor to be faithful to the Gospel, and it must be seen that she is poor." John Paul II made a statement of policy on similar lines: "The primary base for the support of the Apostolic See must be constituted by the spontaneous offerings made by Catholics throughout the world, and possibly also be other men of goodwill. This attitude follows a long Christian tradition which draws its origins from the Gospel (Lk 10:7) and from the teachings of the Apostles (1 Cor 9:11-14). Conforming to this tradition - which has assumed different forms down the centuries of Church history, adapting to the economic and social structures of the times - the Apostolic See can and must use the offerings made by the faithful and other men of good will, without having recourse to other means which could appear less respectful of her peculiar character." John Paul II thinks that the Vatican should be a "house of glass" with no secrets. Any signs of this ideal in practice? When the bribery scandal broke, word immediately reached the Italian magistrates examining the case that the IOR would fully co-operate with them: which was done. It was not a repetition of the crashed Banco Ambrosiano, when the public were left guessing.

The ensure implementation of the papal policy a "vigilance" committee of Cardinals was set up: Cardinals Angelo Sodano (Secretary of State), Bernardin Gantin, John O'Connor, Martinez Somalo, Jose Rosario Castillo Lara. To keep watch on the IOR a number of laymen, experienced in the financial world and of proved integrity, have been brought in: Angelo Caloia, president of the supervisory council; he is a former director of Mediocredito Lombardo: Andrea Gibellini, director; he is counsellor to the Banco Popolare of Bergamo, president of the Christian Union of Entrepreneurs and Directors; Philippe de Weck, vice-president; he is a former president of the *Union des Banques Suisses*, former vice-president of Nestlé; Virgil Deschant, head of the Knights of Columbus; Jose-Sanchez Asianin, he is co-president of the Banco de Bilbao-Vizcaya; Theodor Pietzcher, he is a former director of the Deutche-Bank.

The most important office set up by Paul VI was the Prefecture for the Economic Affairs of the Holy See. The head of this office has the task of "co-ordinating all the administrations of the Holy See's property and exercising supervision over them." The function has been described by the present incumbent, Cardinal Edmund Casimir Szoka, as a combination of the budget office of the Holy See and general accounts of the Holy See. Thus all expenditure is rigidly supervised and, if need be, controlled.

Vatican finances have been running at a deficit in recent years, from 1970. What is

goes in the Catholic Church one finds literature recording the events of the papal visit, the full texts of the addresses given by the Pope, souvenirs of one kind or another, all of which accentuates consciousness of the mystical body, facilitates an ever deeper awareness of communion. The Pope in each region or country has spoken of local needs and problems. There is thus constituted a monumental documentation on the Church in our time. He does not shrink from pointing to error, but he does certainly bring the tonic of Christian hope, the reality of eschatological fulfilment. A whole new generation is growing up worldwide with personal memories of the Head of the Church, with the possibility of openness to any and every challenge which touches their loyalty.

Episcopal conferences coming to Rome are also heartened in the knowledge that the Pope is aware of conditions, difficulties, opportunities in their jurisdiction, which no predecessor of his could have known in the same way.

It was fortunate for the Church, providential to speak with the candour of faith, that the man called to such a mission had physical and nervous stamina, stamina not impaired by the attempted attack on his life. He has had to endure abrupt changes of climate and weather, sudden raising or lowering of altitude, long journeys by plane with no hope of respite or rest on arrival, incessant demands on his linguistic talent; he has shown in his Easter addresses the ability to use - admittedly for short greetings, over fifty languages. How many has he practised in talking to people of the five continents?

He also meets representatives of the world religions, in the spirit of Vatican II, as he everywhere meets representatives of the Jewish communities. It is in the spirit of Assisi (qv), but with all the sound theology of missionary idealism and activity taught in his Encyclical *Redemptoris Missio*. The precept of the Master to Peter was "Preach the good news to all nations" this in common with the other Apostles, and "Feed my lambs, feed my sheep", this to himself in his own office. If any Pope in history has undertaken evangelization and teaching, the substantive duties of the office, it is John Paul II.

Health

John Paul II showed little effect of accidents which befell him in his youth, nor of the restricted diet of the war years. Torn from his university and sent to work in a stone quarry, he may have gained from the outdoor life, as from work in the Solway factory. His episcopal status did not inhibit robust physical exercise, cycling, canoeing, skiing. He often cycled to Czestochowa. Cardinal Jacques Martin, a long time member of the Curia, reports, in his Memoirs, the Pope's words as he entered the Vatican to take up residence, "That's an end to skiing and canoeing." Not altogether, for he did, since becoming Pope, once take a skiing holiday in the Italian alps; he invited the president of Italy to accompany him. Soon after his election he had made two requests - for a set of Stations of the Cross (which was offered by the Irish bishops) and for a swimming pool. When told that the latter would be costly, he replied that a third conclave would cost more - two had just taken place within eight weeks.

The assassination attempt on 13 May, 1981 temporarily weakened him. What really set him back for some time was a virus which he got later; it baffled doctors and may have been caused by contaminated blood given him in a transfusion. On 15 July, 1992, the Pope underwent a surgical operation for an abdominal tumour, "as big as an orange", which should have been diagnosed much earlier. It was declared benign, but later there was talk of "cancerous elements."

On 11 November, 1993, the Pope stumbled and fell descending steps at a general audience. He sustained an injury to the shoulder which yielded to treatment. It is not clear what his present health condition is, that is in the first quarter of the year 1994. People tried to dissuaded him from crossing the Atlantic for the fifth centenary of America after his illness in July 1992. A rest out of Rome helped him recuperate. Presently he has slightly varying states of health even, it would appear, in the course of a single day. But he maintains a demanding schedule.

Humanae Vitae

The year 1993 marked the twenty fifth anniversary of Paul VI's (qv) Encyclical on marriage and the family, 25 July, 1968. Pope John Paul II spoke words of recommendation, praising the wisdom of his predecessor's teaching. The Encyclical, as is well known, forbade the use of contraceptives. What, one may ask, was the reaction of the Archbishop of Cracow, at the time of the Encyclical? He was a member of the papal commission on population, the family and births, the advisory body so much discussed at the time. It was known that when it came to a final vote, a majority favoured allowing contraception. The Pope did not follow them.

Why, it has been asked, was Cardinal Wojtyla absent from the 1966 meeting of the commission, the final one when a vote was taken? How would he have voted? The first question is easily answered. It was the Millennium year in Poland. The Cardinal in Warsaw was under appalling, totally unjust, pressure from the government (see article *Poland*). The other bishops, led by Wojtyla, felt obliged to stand by him, to defend him, which they did in a magnificent letter. None of them, least of all the Archbishop of Cracow, second in dignity, could be away from the scene of battle. Therefore he was not in Rome.

The answer to the second question is easily forthcoming. Already in 1960 the future Pope had published a book which expressed his views on the subject. This work was translated into Italian and French; the French translation appeared with an introduction by the greatest French theologian of the century, Henri (later Cardinal) de Lubac, SJ. The author sought to enlighten modern problems about sexuality with Christian idealism, with the personalist philosophy which was the core of his thinking.

In 1969 the Polish bishops issued a pastoral on the papal Encyclical; Cardinal Wojtyla had certainly worked on it. In the same year he published an *Introduction to Humanae Vitae*; in 1976 he gave a lecture on the subject to the Family Institute in Cracow.

The Cardinal was then well equipped to participate in the international conference held in Milan in June, 1978, four months before his election as Pope. He was a principal speaker. The occasion was the tenth anniversary of *Humanae Vitae*. The other speaker was Fr G Martelet, SJ, who was thought to have worked on the draft of the Encyclical. The meeting was attended by 350 representatives from fifty-seven countries, including thirty-seven Third World Countries.

The text of Cardinal Wojtyla's lecture, "Love and Responsiblity" a personalist, idealistic doctrine of conjugal love, was widely diffused. The Pope gave a remarkable series of talks during 1979 on the theology of sex and Christian marriage.

Jews, The

Joseph Lichten, representative in Rome of the American Jewish Association, B'nai B'rith issued a statement soon after the election of John Paul II, on what he had done as a young man during the Jewish massacre. As an active participant in a clandestine relief organisation, *Unia*, he had given assistance to the Jews in the Cracow area. He helped them to find hiding-places, saving them from deportation and death. When, after the war, he himself could come out of hiding - he was a marked man, protected by Cardinal Sapieha - he identified with the remnant of the Wadowice Jewish community. He was a lifelong friend of one member of the Jewish community, Jerzy Kluger, whose father was president of the decimated ethnic group. The young Wojtyla helped restore the Jewish cemetery. Another boyhood friend of his, Jerzy Zubrzycki, a Professor in Australia, at the time of the election, also gave testimony to his compassion and help for the stricken Jews.

Innovation has marked the policy of John Paul II in regard to the Jewish people. Isolated incidents which did not affect this policy were given some prominence in the press. In 1982 the Pope received Yasir Arafat. In doing so he took no stand whatever in political matters. When he also received Kurt Waldheim, he was dealing with the elected president of Austria, one of the oldest Catholic countries in the world; and incidentally a former Secretary General of the United Nations. When he beatified Edith Stein (in religious life the Carmelite Sister Benedicta of the Holy Cross) he was not intruding on the loyalties of the Jewish people but honouring her commitment to her vocation; it was as a Catholic Jewess that she had, in reprisal for the Dutch Bishops' condemnation of the Nazi anti-semitic programme, been made prisoner and sent to Auschwitz (qv).

John Paul II has supported the Council of Christians and Jews and the Vatican Commission for Religious Relations with the Jews, which were established before his election, as he supported the International Jewish-Christian Conference on Religious Leadership in Christian Society which was held in Jerusalem in February, 1994; and as he approved the Vatican Publication "Notes on the correct way to present the Jews and Judaism in Preaching and Catechesis", 1985. The Pope welcomes meetings with Jewish representatives: in Mainz, Germany in 1980, in Castelgandolfo, and in Miami in 1987.

On 13 April, 1986 John Paul II took the unprecedented step of visiting the Jewish Synagogue in Rome. He spoke to his audience in the sacred language of their religious traditions, evoking the "Holy One of Israel", recalling the anguish which he had expressed at Auschwitz (qv). In 1992 he also received the Foreign Minister of Israel, Shimon Peres, who as Prime Minister had visited him in 1985; this time he invited the Pope to Israel. Much more important was the visit to the Pope of the Chief Rabbi of Israel, Yisrael Meir Lau, on 21 September, 1993. This was the first visit of such a high religious dignitary to the Pope - the first Chief Rabbi, Isaac Halevi Herzog, had been received by Pius XII, as he was on his way to take up his office - so he told me in 1957. A recent Chief Rabbi had refused to see the Pope. Rabbi Meir Lsu expressed his feelings thus: "He would be very welcome in my house. I will welcome him with friends and help and warmth."

The culmination of John Paul's activity on behalf of the Jewish people came with the agreement between the Vatican and the State of Israel. With the Pope's active encouragement the negotiations had been conducted since 1992. They ended with the signature on 30 December, 1993 of the Fundamental Agreement, which guarantees freedom of worship and conscience, and opens the way for full diplomatic relations between the two states. Commenting on it in his New Year's address to the Diplomatic Corps, the Pope also sated that he would press for recognition of Palestinian rights. Soon after negotiations were begun between the Vatican and the PLO. The first papal envoy has been appointed to Israel, to prepare for the establishment of ambassadors. He has since received the Israeli Prime Minister, Mr Rabim, in audience.

In the same general context of sympathy for the Jewish people a special message sent to the Apostolic Nuncio in Warsaw on the 19 April, 1993 was noteworthy. Through his representative the Pope sent his sympathy and support to the celebration organised by the Polish president, Lech Walesa, to commemorate the fiftieth anniversary of the Jewish rising in the ghetto against the occupying forces. Present were the Prime Minister of Israel and important Jews from all over the world.

When John XXIII voiced his sympathy for Jews - "I am your brother, Joseph" to Jewish visitors - and Vatican II developed his intuition in formal teaching, all this came from outside, wholly admirable as it was. John Paul II grew up in a country with one of the largest Jewish minorities in the whole world - over three million in Warsaw alone. In a sense he and they belong to each other. He has been worthy of the trust.

It is of interest to note the opening section of the Fundamental Agreement between the Holy See and the State of Israel, which I quote here below:

> **Mindful** of the singular character and universal significance of the Holy Land.
> **Aware** of the unique nature of the relationship between the Catholic Church and the Jewish people, and of the historic process of reconciliation and growth in the mutual understanding and friendship between Catholics and Jews.
> **Having decided** on 29 July 1992 to establish and "Bilateral Permanent Working Commission", in order to study and define together issues of common interest, and in view of normalizing their relations.
> **Recognizing** that the work of the aforementioned Commission has produced sufficient material for a first and Fundamental Agreement.
> **Realizing** that such Agreement will provide a sound and lasting basis for the continued development of their present and future relations and for the furtherance of the Commission's task,
> **Agree** upon the following articles:
>
> **Article 1**
> 1. The State of Israel, recalling its Declaration of Independence, affirms its continuing commitment to uphold and observe the human right to freedom of religion and conscience, as set forth in the Universal Declaration of Human Rights and in other international instruments to which it is a party.
> 2. The Holy See, recalling the Declaration on Religious Freedom of the Second Vatican Council, *Dignitatis humanae*, affirms the Catholic Church's commitment to uphold the human right to freedom of religion and conscience as set forth in the Universal Declaration of Human Rights and in other international instruments to which it is a party. The Holy See wishes to affirm as well the Catholic Church's respect for other religions and their followers as solemnly stated by the Second Vatican Ecumenical Council in its Declaration on the Relation of the Church to Non-Christian Religions, *Nostra aetate*.

Article 2

1. The Holy See and the State of Israel are committed to appropriate cooperation in combatting all forms of anti-semitism and all kinds of racism and of religious intolerance, and in promoting mutual understanding among nations, tolerance among communities and respect for human life and dignity.

2. The Holy See takes this occasion to reiterate its condemnation of hatred, persecution and all other manifestations of anti-semitism directed against the Jewish people and individual Jews anywhere, at any time and by anyone. In particular, the Holy See deplores attacks on Jews and desecration of Jewish synagogues and cemeteries, acts which offend the memory of the victims of the Holocaust, especially when they occur in the same places which witnessed it.

Article 3

1. The Holy See and the State of Israel recognize that both are free in the exercise of their respective rights and powers, and commit themselves to respect this principle in their mutual relations and in their cooperation for the good of the people.

2. The State of Israel recognizes the right of the Catholic Church to carry out its religious, moral, educational and charitable functions, and to have its own institutions, and to train, appoint and deploy its own personnel in the said institutions or for the said functions to these ends. The Church recognizes the right of the State to carry out its functions, such as promoting and protecting the welfare and the safety of the people. Both the Sate and the Church recognize the need for dialogue and cooperation in such matters as by their nature call for it.

3. Concerning Catholic legal personality at canon law the Holy See and the State of Israel will negotiate on giving it full effect in Israeli law, following a report from a joint subcommission of experts.

Article 4

1. The State of Israel affirms its continuing commitment to maintain and respect the "Status quo" in the Christian Holy Places to which it applies and the respective rights of the Christian communities thereunder. The Holy See affirms the Catholic Church's continuing commitment to respect the aforementioned "Status quo" and the said rights.

2. The above shall apply notwithstanding an interpretation to the contrary of any Article in this Fundamental Agreement.

Joseph, Saint

The modern Papacy, since Pius IX, has been committed to promoting the cult of St Joseph; this Pope, in 1870, proclaimed him Patron of the Universal Church and in 1889 Leo XIII, in the Encyclical *Quamquam Pluries*, summarized the theology of the

was restored to life in 1956 and appeared normally from 1957. Today, enrolment at the University is at over 10,000.

Mary, Mother of God

John Paul II is a Marian Pope. In his first Encyclical, *Redemptor Hominis*, he wrote thus:

> Since Paul VI, inspired by that teaching (ie, of Vatican II) proclaimed the Mother of Christ 'Mother of the Church' and that title has become known far and wide, may it be permitted to his unworthy successor to turn to Mary as Mother of the Church at the close of these reflections which it was opportune to make at the beginning of his papal service. Mary is Mother of the Church because, on account of the Eternal Father's ineffable choice, and due to the Spirit of the Lord's special action, she gave human life to the Son of God, 'for whom and by whom all things exist' (Heb 2:10) and from whom the whole of the People of God receives the grace and dignity of election.

The Pope went on to recall Mary's spiritual motherhood of men, manifest in the word of Christ from the Cross, her closeness to the Holy Spirit in expectation of his descent at Pentecost, the wish today's disciples of Christ have to unite themselves with her. "We do so" he writes, "with all our attachment to our ancient tradition and also with full respect and love for the members of all the Christian communities."

With this ecumenical gesture he turns to the mystery of the Redemption, our need at the present time. "We believe" he writes:

> that nobody else can bring us as Mary can into the divine and human aspect of this mystery. Nobody has been brought into it by God as Mary has. It is in this that the exceptional character of the grace of the divine Motherhood consists. Not only is the dignity of this Motherhood unique and unrepeatable in the history of the human race, but Mary's participation, due to this Maternity, in God's plan for man's salvation through the mystery of the Redemption is also unique in profundity and range of action. We can say that the mystery of the Redemption took shape beneath the heart of the Virgin of Nazareth.

From this beginning the Pope has gone on to a continuous, manifold exposition of Marian theology and spirituality, accompanied by a manifestation of piety, official and personal, that makes the pontificate distinctive even by comparison with other recent Popes - Pius XII alone excepted, for he is unrivalled in Marian doctrine and devotion. Practically every important papal text issued since John Paul II was elected has a passage related to Our Lady, often by way of conclusion. One expects this in teaching on the Missions, for Marian institutes have had a significant role in the modern missionary movement. One expects it too in *Mulieris Dignitatem*, on the feminist question, noting nevertheless that the chapter on Mary, ideal woman, model of her sex, is given prominence and substance.

The point is that throughout the whole corpus of teaching, the Pope is seen to turn to Mary as inspiration or intercessor or model. It is well known that he has visited Marian shrines everywhere his pastoral journeys have taken him. He has rejoiced in honouring great servants of Our Lady, like St Maximilian Kolbe, his fellow-countryman, and Juan Diego, the visionary of Guadalupe. It is also well known that he loves to recite the Rosary on radio - his first gesture holding it aloft to the public soon after his election, was noteworthy. (See articles *Apparitions of Our Lady*, *Alliance of the Two Hearts* and *Russia*).

John Paul II is a powerful current of theological speculation which has emerged since Vatican II on the relationship between Mary and the Holy Spirit (see article, *Spirit, The Holy and Mary, Mother of God*). The student of his Marian theology will, however, pay special attention to the Encyclical Letter, *Redemptoris Mater*, 25 March, 1987, on the occasion of a Marian Year declared by the Pope from Pentecost Sunday, 7 June, 1987 to the Feast of the Assumption, 15 August, 1988.

The Encyclical has certain distinctive features. One is the analysis of Mary's faith in the light of biblical witness, more lengthily than had been done in previous church documents. The Pope deals also with Christian Unity and Mary's role therein, referring especially to the Orthodox (qv). He seeks to reopen the question of Mary's mediation, which was not treated to everyone's satisfaction by Vatican II (qv). In a first schema, that is draft conciliar text, Our Lady's universal mediation had been clearly affirmed. When the Council had voted to deal with her not in a separate constitution, (the name of basic doctrinal statements) but in a chapter of that on the Church, a new draft text was ordered. It was brought to the assembly for discussion in September, 1964. There was opposition not only to the idea of Mary's universal mediation, but to the very word Mediatress. A compromise formula was put forward; Mary "is invoked in the Church under the titles of Advocate, Helper, Benefactress and Mediatress." Up to the last day of the debate there were some Fathers led by a Cardinal, Alfrink of Holland, who sought the deletion of the word. True, the statement which looks merely empirical, is buttressed by other considerations.

Looming over all the discord was the ecumenical concern, but ecumenical almost, at this point, exclusively in a Protestant perspective. This explained errors and partiality in the preliminaries to the final vote on the conciliar text. Partiality: when a great Byzantine scholar, Fr A Wenger, AA submitted a memorandum to the drafting commission on the importance of Mary's mediatorial role for the Easterns, including the Orthodox, he was told to practise moderation, that is to forget the relevant history of theology! Errors: in an official report distributed among the Fathers to enlighten them there were two howlers. It was stated that Pius XII never used the title Mediatress; he did so eight times. It was stated that the Easterns used the title, but not in a systematic way; the most remarkable synthesis on the subject is from an Orthodox pen, Theophanes of Nicaea (d.1381). Apparently to reassure Protestants, the one Mediator proclaimed by St Paul is several times affirmed, directly or indirectly.

John Paul II as always shows the greatest respect for the conciliar text; he tries to extract its maximum content. But he makes the affirmation more explicit:

> With the redeeming death of her Son, the maternal mediation of the handmaid of the Lord took on a universal dimension, for the work of redemption embraces the whole of humanity. Thus there is manifested in a singular way the efficacy of the one and universal mediation of Christ 'between God and man.' Mary's co-operation shares, in its subordinate character, in the universality of the mediation of the Redeemer, the Mediator.

The Catholic Church went through, after Vatican II, what a great biblical scholar and Marian theologian, Ignace de la Potterie, SJ called (at the International Mariological Congress in Huelva, September, 1992), "a decade without Mary", slightly hyperbolic but thought-provoking. We should put it between 1965 and 1974 when Paul VI published his Apostolic Exhortation, *Marialis Cultus*. The Council teaching was scarcely responsible for this abrupt decline from the great Marian age of Pius XII, who had consecrated the world to the Immaculate Heart of Mary, declared two Marian Years, defined solemnly the dogma of the Assumption, and proclaimed the universal queenship of Mary - these events within a constant flow of instruction and devotion.

If the Council teaching was not to blame, possibly certain events in its history, open to malicious misinterpretation should be judged: the vote on the place of the Marian text showed a split almost fifty fifty per cent, with a majority less than two per cent favouring inclusion within the Constitution on the Church. Though the question at issue, as was made clear on the day of the vote, was procedural, the view could be spread about that the Catholic Church, at least half of it, was on a back-track in regard to Our Lady. Again the confrontation in the debate on the Marian text seemed almost like bishops quarrelling about the Mother of God! Even the wholly unjustifiable exclusion of St Joseph (qv) could be wrongly exploited.

We have seen the return of Mary, Mother of God. Paul VI strove to rectify things. It is his present successor who has really set the Church on the right course. Nor must we forget that Our Lady herself has intervened decisively in the life of the pilgrim Church (see article *Apparitions*). A most willing instrument in the working of the Holy Spirit who is everywhere active is John Paul II.

The Pope will in the near future be offered the results of a worldwide consultation of bishops, priests, religious, laity on the titles Co-redemptress, Advocate, Mediatress. He will be respectfully asked to define these truths as dogmas of the faith. At the present rate of progress the consultation may result in fifty million signatures. A group of scholars are preparing a work which will show the validity of the titles.

Mercy, Reconciliation and Penance

John Paul II is the first Pope in modern times who goes down to St Peter's Basilica at certain times and is available as a confessor.

Those who think that in doctrine he is too unyielding may advert to this fact. But they should especially read two important documents which he has published: his Encyclical on divine mercy, *Dives in Misericordia*, 2 December 1980 and the Apostolic Exhortation, *Reconciliatio et Paenitentia*, 2 December, 1984. The second document was based on the work of the Sixth General Assembly of the Synod of Bishops, convoked by the Pope, and on the advice of many bishops given the theme: *Reconciliation and Penance in the Mission of the Church*. The Pope also made reconciliation the centre of the Jubilee Year called to celebrate the 1950th anniversary of the Redemption.

The two papal texts read together afford a penetrating analysis of the sinfulness of contemporary society, of the means available to those who take the essential decision and seek reconciliation, of the immense resources within the Church to ensure renewal and above all of the ultimate hope of the sinner, infinite divine mercy: the key sentence in the Encyclical is that mercy comes from "a love more powerful than sin, stronger than death." The Pope exhorts all who believe in one God, Christians, Moslems, Jews, to imitate the Father's mercy.

A quotation from the Apostolic Exhortation will summarize the Pope's thought and hope:

> This exhortation is completely permeated by words which Peter heard from Jesus himself, and by ideas which formed part of this 'Good News': the new commandment of love of neighbour; the yearning for and commitment to unity; the beatitudes of mercy and patience in persecution for the sake of justice; the repaying of evil with good; the forgiveness of offenses; the love of enemies. In these words and ideas is the original and transcendent synthesis of the Christian ethic, or more accurately and more profoundly, of the spirituality of the New Covenant in Jesus Christ.

I entrust to the Father, rich in mercy, I entrust to the Son of God, made man as our Redeemer and Reconciler, I entrust to the Holy Spirit, source of unity and peace, this call of mine, as father and pastor, to penance and reconciliation. May the Most Holy and Adorable Trinity cause to spring up in the Church and in the world the small seed which at this hour I plant in the generous soil of many hearts.

In order that in the not too distant future abundant fruits may come from it, I invite you all to join me in turning to Christ's Heart, the eloquent sign of the divine mercy, the 'propitiation for our sins', 'our peace and reconciliation' (Litany of the Sacred Heart, cf 1 Jn 2:2; Eph 2:14; Rm 3:25; 5:11) that we may draw from it an interior encouragement to hate sin and to be converted in God, and find in it the divine kindness which lovingly responds to human repentance. "I likewise invite you to turn with me to the Immaculate Heart of Mary, Mother of Jesus, in whom is effected the reconciliation of God with humanity.. is accomplished the work of reconciliation, because she has received from God the fullness of grace in virtue of the redemptive sacrifice of Christ. (The Pope's words 7 December, 1983). Truly, Mary has been associated with God, by virtue of her divine Motherhood, in the work of reconciliation.

Into the hands of this Mother, whose 'Fiat' marked the beginning of that 'fullness of time' in which Christ accomplished the reconciliation of humanity with God, to her Immaculate Heart - to which we have repeatedly entrusted the whole of humanity, disturbed by sin and tormented by so many tensions and conflicts - I now in a special way entrust this intention: that through her intercession humanity may discover and travel the path of penance, the only path that can lead to full reconciliation.

Missions, The

The Catholic Missions present a puzzling picture. Two thousand years after he lived, Jesus Christ, Saviour of all humankind, is unknown to more than two thirds of those whom he lived and died and rose from the dead to save. The Popes of the present century have been very conscious of the need of a missionary policy. A series of Encyclicals and similar documents express their deeply felt concern in this area. Have the results been such as would respond to their desires?

These words of John Paul II must be weighed in answering this question:

The number of those who do not know Christ and do not belong to the Church is constantly on the increase. Indeed since the end of the Council it has almost doubled.

Since the Pope refers to the Council let us recall a little history. Vatican II expressed its teaching in a series of documents, Constitutions, Decrees, Declarations. One of the subjects to be dealt with was the Church's missionary activity. At one moment in the history of the conciliar sessions it was not deemed worthy of the greatest attention. Whereas other subjects were deemed worthy of substantial texts, the Missions were being dealt with in a series of propositions, which by their form could not express a very profound theology. In face of protests there was a change and in the end an impressive document was drafted, amended and passed.

There was another problem. The Declaration on Religious Liberty and the Decree on the Church and the World Religions could be misread to allege lack of importance in the Church's evangelizing mission. This was not the note struck loud and clear in the Encyclicals of Benedict XV, Pius XI, Pius XII, John XXIII and in the Apostolic Exhortation of Paul VI. The Pope's meeting with world religious leaders in Assisi (qv) could be likewise misunderstood.

John Paul II has laboured much, and travelled much to show the importance of the Church's missionary vocation, in addresses for world mission day and to missionary institutes. He has especially shown his commitment to the ideal in his extensive pastoral visits to the young churches facing the task of evangelization or of re-evangelization. In this respect he is the outstanding missionary Pope of all time since St Peter.

The Pope has clarified teaching on the subject in his Encyclical, *Redemptoris Missio*, 7 December, 1990; the date was the twenty-fifth anniversary of the conciliar decrees, *Ad Gentes*. John Paul wished to remove all doubt, hesitancy, ambiguity on the Church's mission *ad gentes* to the nations of the whole world. He was concerned to affirm that Jesus Christ is the Saviour of all. He was concerned to afford advice on particularly urgent needs at the present time, such as ecclesial basic communities, incarnating the Gospel in native cultures. Here he recalled two fundamental principals: inculturation must be compatible with the Gospel and be in communion with the entire Church.

In regard to missionary activity the Pope insisted that the proclamation of Christ is the absolute primary imperative, a logical conclusion from the universality of his saving mission. He dealt with the elaborate practical elements needed in the fulfilment of the missionary vocation to which all are called by Baptism; he outlined a spirituality of mission.

As a foundation for all these considerations Pope John Paul set forth a theology of mission. Here, with the primacy of Christ and his universal saving mission, there are two key concepts, the Kingdom of God and the role of the Holy Spirit (qv). The relationship of the Church to the kingdom is explained. On the Holy Spirit John Paul II has brought to a certain plenitude an idea that was thought of by those who drafted the revised conciliar scheme on the missionary activity of the Church. They did not develop this idea at length. Paul VI in *Evangelii Nuntiandi* (an Apostolic Exhortation published after the Third General Synod, held in 1974 - the text was issued a year later, 8 December, 1975) introduces a section of the document with the words: "There can be no evangelization without the co-operation of the Holy Spirit." He then outlines the significant events in the life of Christ and offers some reflections on Pentecost. He ends with these words:

> The Synod of bishops which was held in 1974 after it had duly stressed the action of the Holy Spirit in the work of evangelization, declared that the pastors of souls and theologians - and we may include also the faithful who have received the seal of the Holy Spirit in Baptism - should study in greater depth the nature and manner of the action of the Holy Spirit in evangelization in these times.

Among those present at this important synod was the future John Paul II. (See article *Cracow*).

In Chapter Three of the Encyclical *Redemptoris Missio* he shows his response to the request of the Synod, of which he himself was a member. The chapter is reproduced in full to exemplify a principal thesis of this whole book, that John Paul II is the apostle of the Holy Spirit to our times:

> At the climax of Jesus' messianic mission, the Holy Spirit becomes present in the Paschal Mystery in all of his divine subjectivity: as the one who is now to continue the salvific work rooted in the sacrifice of the Cross. Of course, Jesus entrusts this work to human beings: to the Apostles, to the Church. Nevertheless, in and through them the Holy Spirit remains the transcendent and principal agent for the accomplishment of this work in the human spirit and in the history of the world... [1]

> All the Evangelists, when they describe the Risen Christ's meeting with his Apostles, conclude with the "missionary mandate": "All authority in heaven and on earth has been given to me. Go therefore and make disciples of all nations... and lo, I am with you always, to the close of the age" (Mt 28:18-20; cf. Mk 16:15-18; Lk 24:46-49; Jn 20:21-23).

> This is *a sending forth in the Spirit*, as is clearly apparent in the Gospel of John: Christ sends his own into the world, just as the Father has sent him, and to this end he gives them the Spirit. Luke, for his part, closely links the witness the Apostles are to give to Christ with the working of the Spirit, who will enable them to fulfil the mandate they have received...

---

[1] Encyclical Letter <u>Dominum et Vivificantem</u> (18 May 1986), 42: <u>AAS</u> 78 (1986), 857.

'And they went forth and preached everywhere, while the Lord worked with them' (Mk 16:20)... The mission of the Church, like that of Jesus, is God's work or, as Luke often puts it, the work of the Spirit. After the Resurrection and Ascension of Jesus, the Apostles have a powerful experience which completely transforms them: the experience of Pentecost. The coming of the Holy Spirit makes them *witnesses* and *prophets* (cf. Acts 1:8; 2:17-18). It fills them with a serene courage which impels them to pass on to others their experience of Jesus and the hope which motivates them. The Spirit gives them the ability to bear witness to Jesus with "boldness"... [1]

Paul and Barnabas are impelled by the Spirit to go to the Gentiles (cf. Acts 13:46-48), a development not without certain tensions and problems. How are these converted Gentiles to live their faith in Jesus? Are they bound by the traditions of Judaism and the law of circumcision? At the first Council, which gathers the members of the different Churches together with the Apostles in Jerusalem, a decision is taken which is acknowledged as coming from the Spirit: it is not necessary for a Gentile to submit to the Jewish Law in order to become a Christian (cf. Acts 15:5-11, 28). From now on the Church opens her doors and becomes the house which all may enter, and in which all can feel at home, while keeping their own culture and traditions, provided that these are not contrary to the Gospel.

The missionaries continued along this path, taking account of people's hopes and expectations, their anguish and sufferings, as well as their culture, in order to proclaim to them salvation in Christ... But if they are to recognize the true God, they must abandon the false gods which they themselves have made and open themselves to the One whom God has sent to remedy their ignorance and satisfy the longings of their hearts.

One of the central purposes of mission is to bring people together in hearing the Gospel, in fraternal communion, in prayer and in the Eucharist. To live in "fraternal communion" (*koinonia*) means to be "of one heart and soul" (Acts 4:23), establishing fellowship from every point of view: human, spiritual and material. Indeed, a true Christian community is also committed to distributing earthly goods, so that no one is in want, and all can receive such goods "as they need" (cf. Acts 2:45; 4:35). The first communities, made up of "glad and generous hearts" (Acts 2:46), were open and missionary: they enjoyed "favour with all the people" (Acts 2:47). Even before activity, mission means witness and a way of life that shines out to others...[2]

---

[1] The greek word "parrhesia" also means enthusiasm or energy; cf. Acts 2:29; 4:13, 29,31; 9:27-28; 13:46; 14:3; 18:26; 19:8,26; 28:31.
[2] Cf. PAUL VI, Apostolic Exhortation Evangelii Nuntiandi, 41-42: loc. cit., 31-33.

Reading the Acts of the Apostles helps us to realize that at the beginning of the Church the mission *ad gentes*, while it had missionaries dedicated "for life" by a special vocation, was in fact considered the normal outcome of Christian living, to which every believer was committed through the witness of personal conduct and through explicit proclamation whenever possible.

The Spirit manifests himself in a special way in the Church and in her members. Nevertheless, his presence and activity are universal, limited neither by space nor time.[1] The Second Vatican Council recalls that the Spirit is at work in the heart of every person...[2]

The Spirit's presence and activity affect not only individuals but also society and history, peoples, cultures and religions. Indeed, the Spirit is at the origin of the noble ideals and undertakings which benefit humanity on its journey through history: "The Spirit of God with marvellous foresight directs the course of the ages and renews the face of the earth."[3] The Risen Christ "is now at work in human hearts through the strength of his Spirit, not only instilling a desire for the world to come but also thereby animating, purifying and reinforcing the noble aspirations which drive the human family to make its life one that is more human and to direct the whole earth to this end."[4] Again, it is the Spirit who sows the "seeds of the Word" present in various customs and cultures, preparing them for full maturity in Christ[5]...

The Church's relationship with other religions is dictated by a twofold respect: "Respect for man in his quest for answers to the deepest questions of his life, and respect for the action of the Spirit in man."[6] Excluding any mistaken interpretation, the inter-religious meeting held in Assisi was meant to confirm my conviction that "every authentic prayer is prompted by the Holy Spirit, who is mysteriously present in every human heart"...[7]

Whatever the Spirit brings about in human hearts and in the history of peoples,

---

[1]Cf. Encyclical Letter **Dominum et Vivificantem**, 53: loc. cit., 874f.

[2]Cf. "Second Vatican Ecumenical Council", Decree on the Missionary Activity of the Church **Ad Gentes**, 3, 11, 15.

[3]"Second Vatican Ecumenical Council", Pastoral Constitution on the Church in the World of Today **Gaudium et Spes**, 26.

[4]Ibid.,38; cf.93.

[5]Cf. "Second Vatican Ecumenical Council", Dogmatic Constitution on the Church **Lumen Gentium**, 17.

[6]Address to Representatives of Non-Christian Religions, Madras, 5 February 1986: **AAS** 78 (1986), 767; cf. **Message to the Peoples of Asia**, Manila, 21 February 1981, 2-4: **AAS** 73 (1981), 392f; Address to Representatives of Other Religions, Tokyo, 24 February 1981, 3-4: **Insegnamenti** IV/I (1981), 507f.

[7]Address to Cardinals and the Roman Curia, 22 December 1986, 11: **AAS** 79 (1987), 1089.

in cultures and religions serves as a preparation for the Gospel[1] and can only be understood in reference to Christ, the Word who took flesh by the power of the Spirit "so that as perfectly human he would save all human beings and sum up all things."[2]

Moreover, the universal activity of the Spirit is not to be separated from his particular activity within the Body of Christ, which is the Church. Indeed, it is always the Spirit who is at work, both when he gives life to the Church and impels her to proclaim Christ, and when he implants and develops his gifts in all individuals and peoples, guiding the Church to discover these gifts, to foster them and receive them through dialogue. Every form of the Spirit's presence is to be welcomed with respect and gratitude, but the discernment of this presence is the responsibility of the Church (cf. Jn 16:13).

Our own time, with humanity on the move and in continual search, demands *a resurgence of the Church's missionary activity*. The horizons and possibilities for mission are growing ever wider, and we Christians are called to an apostolic courage based upon trust in the Spirit...

Opus Dei

An association mostly of Catholic lay people, but with a number of priest members, dedicated to the highest Christian ideals, with notable ascetic spirit and discipline. It was founded in Madrid on 2 October, 1928, by Jose Maria Escrivá de Balaguer, a Spanish priest with varied pastoral experience. It has spread widely through the five continents into eighty nations, recruiting membership among the professional classes, with a preponderance of upper middle class members. It undertakes publishing, specializes in education, especially in institutes of higher learning including universities. The spirituality is contained in the writings of the founder, succinctly and lucidly conveyed in *The Way*, which has already sold well over three and a half million copies. It is staunchly loyal to the Church, to the sacred traditions, to the Papacy. Its value in this commitment has been appreciated and rewarded by John Paul II. In 1982 he granted the association the first personal prelature in the history of the Catholic Church, with a legal position within the hierarchy. The first member named to this post was Mgr Alvaro del Portillo.

---

[1] Cf. "Second Vatican Ecumenical Council", Dogmatic Constitution on the Church Lumen Gentium, 16.
[2] "Second Vatican Ecumenical Council", Pastoral Constitution on the Church in the World of Today Gaudium et Spes, 45; cf. Encyclical Letter Dominum et Vivificantem, 54: loc. cit., 876.

challenged by the separated churches of the West, the Orthodox are abundant in teaching of the purest, most exalted and erudite kind. Many Catholics will be surprised to hear - it is the judgement of an expert, Fr Martin Jugie, AA - that the greatest theologian of Our Lady's universal mediation is not St Louis Marie Grignion de Montfort, nor St Alphonsus de Liguori, but the Orthodox theologian Theophanes of Nicaea (d.1381). A colleague of Fr Jugie's, Fr Salaville, expert also, has declared that the Byzantine liturgy of Our Lady is the most beautiful ever composed. The *Akathistos* hymn in honour of Our Lady, composed before the break with Rome, acknowledged as the most perfect in Marian hymnography, is an integral part of their liturgy.

What have we to show as progress in Christian unity with the Orthodox in this year when we celebrate the thirtieth anniversary of the *Decree on Ecumenism* promulgated by Vatican II? First, we note the concern of John Paul II, explicitly expressed. In the Encyclical on Our Lady, *Redemptoris Mater*, 25 March, 1987, he made a point of drawing attention to the Orthodox devotion to the Mother of God:

> On the other hand I wish to emphasize how profoundly the Catholic Church, the Orthodox Church and the ancient Churches of the East feel united by love and praise of the *Theotokos* (here the Pope quotes Vatican II). The brethren of these Churches have experienced a complex history, but it is one that has always been marked by an intense desire for Christian commitment and apostolic activity, despite frequent persecution, even to the point of bloodshed. It is a history of fidelity to the Lord, an authentic 'pilgrimage of faith' in space and time, during which Eastern Christians have always looked with boundless trust to the Mother of the Lord, celebrated her with praise and invoked her with unceasing prayer.

The Pope singles out for praise the great eastern Orthodox traditions, Byzantine, Coptic, Ethiopian, Syriac, Armenian. He turns to the important place of icons in that world, describing each of the great categories. His tribute to the Russian Orthodox begins with a reference to the most beautiful icon in the world - an opinion expressed to the writer by a specialist, Paul Evdokimov, author of *La théologie de la beauté*:

> It is also appropriate to mention the icon of Our Lady of Vladimir, which continually accompanied the pilgrimage of faith of the people of ancient Rus'. The first Millennium of the conversion of those noble lands to Christianity is approaching: lands of humble folk, of thinkers and of saints. The Icons are still venerated in the Ukraine, in Byelorussia and in Russia under various titles. They are images which witness to the faith and spirit of prayer of that people, who sense the presence and protection of the Mother of God. In these Icons the Virgin shines as the image of divine beauty, the abode of Eternal Wisdom, the figure of one who prays, the prototype of contemplation, the image of glory: she who in her earthly life possessed the

spiritual knowledge inaccessible to human reasoning and who attained through faith the most sublime knowledge. I also recall the Icon of the Virgin of the Cenacle, praying with the Apostles as they awaited the Holy Spirit; could she not become the sign of hope for all those who, in fraternal dialogue, wish to deepen their obedience of faith? (*Redemptoris Mater*, 31-33)

No Pope has ever spoken like this to the Orthodox. The Pope then made a splendid declaration of hope:

Such a wealth of praise, built up by the different forms of the Church's great tradition, could help us to hasten the day when the Church can begin once more to breathe fully with her two lungs, the East and the West.

Now comes the most important statement, one welcome to those who, like the present writer, have complained of Catholic indifference to the Orthodox:

As I have often said, this is more than ever necessary today.

Why? one may ask. One simple reason is that religion, the Orthodox religion, is coming back in Russia, and Europe presents the image of declining Catholicism. The Pope has another motive:

It would be an effective aid in furthering the progress of dialogue already taking place between the Catholic Church and the Churches and Ecclesial Communities of the West.

For anyone acquainted with the course of ecumenical dialogue between Catholics and Protestants the point made by the Pope will be crystal clear.

A further phase in Orthodox-Catholic relations was reached with the meeting in Balamand, Lebanon, of theologians from both Churches; it took place from 18 to 24 June, 1993, in the theological school of the Greek Patriarchate of Antioch. Speaking to an audience in Rome some days before, John Paul II asked for special prayers to the Holy Spirit. "In December, 1987", he said:

on the occasion of the visit to Rome of our venerable brother, Patriarch Dimitrios, we gave thanks together to the Lord for the firm progress in our common dialogue. On the basis of those results and relying especially on the constant divine assistance, I now express my sincere wish that satisfactory solutions may be found for the question under examination today concerning the relations between the Oriental Catholic Churches and the Orthodox Churches. I invite you to pray with me that the Holy Spirit may enlighten hearts and move people sincerely to seek the paths of full unity which the Lord wants for his disciples. Thus the theological research, which has been so successful until now, can continue. A loyal clarification of the historical controversies in a spirit of ecclesial fraternity and an attitude of obedience to the Lord's will alone, will further the process of theological dialogue in view of full communion and will also point out ways and means to offer henceforth a joint witness of unselfish co-operation in proclaiming the Gospel. During this period of anxiety and tension, as tragic conflicts and fratricidal wars are spreading, the generous commitment of Catholics and Orthodox to intensify their search for full unity will certainly be a real contribution to reconciliation among peoples and to building new relationships of solidarity among the nations. (*OR* 13 June, 1993)

Six months earlier, 15 January, 1993, Pope John Paul had signed an Apostolic Letter, *Europae Orientalis*, establishing the Roman Commission for Eastern Europe. In this he stated, among other things:

The Commission will be responsible for promoting the apostolic mission of the Catholic Church in all her activities and likewise for fostering dialogue with the Orthodox and with other Churches of the eastern tradition. (*OR* 7 March, 1993)

Participants at the Lebanon meeting included twenty-four Catholics, among them Cardinal Cassidy, head of the Vatican Secretariat for Christian Unity, and representatives of nine Orthodox Churches. Orthodox Churches in Serbia, Greece, Bulgaria, the Czech Republic, Georgia and Jerusalem did not send representatives; political disorder impeded the Georgian representative from attending.

A violent incident occurred. A police-escorted bus carrying eighteen Catholic delegates was moving down a mountain-side when a bomb exploded some distance ahead. Two men preparing the blast were killed.

The report issued after the meeting is both reassuring and chilling. Chilling because it stated that relations between Orthodox and Catholics had been "envenomed" (envenimés) by certain initiatives taken in the past. Reassuring because it emphasized the reality that the Orthodox and Catholic Churches are sisters, that neither tends to urge members to change from one to the other, that "uniatism" is rejected.

Uniatism meant the process by which whole groups of Orthodox united with Rome, while preserving their Orthodox heritage. The whole Balamand report is required reading for those interested, in any way, in Christian unity. It removes obstacles, is entirely in the spirit of John Paul II's approach to this problem complicated by so much painful history and theological debate.

Paul VI (1897-1978)

Paul VI had deep attachment to the Polish people and he admired their great leader, Cardinal Wyszynski. As a young papal diplomat he had spent the first six months of his career at the Warsaw nunciature. He had a number of Polish prelates in the Curia, three well known: Cardinal Filipiak, Dean of the Roman Rota, Mgr Ladislaus Rubin, Secretary General of the Episcopal Synod, and Mgr Andrzej Deskur, president of the Papal Commission for Social Communications. Working close to Pius XII, he knew how Poland had suffered during the war. He knew too of Polish valour, witness in Italy itself the military graves on the slopes of Monte Cassino, prominent those of General Anders and the Chaplain General, Bishop Gawlina. Mgr Montini knew that the end of the war had brought no relief to Catholics, as it had done elsewhere. He knew what Wyszynski meant when, as a Cardinal in Rome in 1957 he spoke these words: "Pray for us, we are holding the rampart."

The Pope was to express his admiration for the Cardinal later, in a letter for his sacerdotal Golden Jubilee, in 1974:

> We encourage you, who are hardened in courage and confident in the might of the holy name of Jesus and the victorious Cross, to continue working for the Church.

The Pope also recalled the best known things about the Cardinal, his intense, deep, devotion to Our Lady. During Vatican II, Paul VI had a special request from the Polish bishops to honour Our Lady. The day he proclaimed Mary, Mother of the Church he met Wyszynski and greeted him with these words: "You must be happy now." The Polish bishops had asked for consecration of the world to the Immaculate Heart of Mary, Mother of the Church, by the Pope and all the bishops. Paul VI had wished to honour his friend and the Polish people by visiting the country in the Millenium Year, 1966. At Holy Week and Eastertime I had been in the country and had a wonderful interview with the Cardinal. I said that I might be seeing the Pope some days later. "Tell him we still hope he will come" was his message. When Paul VI heard it he said quite simply, "The government have refused me a visa."

Was there any special bond between Paul VI and the man he named Cardinal on 26 June, 1967, whom he had chosen as Archbishop when two other candidates were being strongly supported? The two men differed very much in temperament, but mutual confidence was strong. Paul VI named the Cardinal to three Roman Congregations, those for Priests, for Divine Worship, and for Catholic Education. He was a consultant to the Papal Council for the Lay Apostolate. Since 1969 he had been a member of the fifteen strong Council of the General Secretariat of the Episcopal Synod. It has been said that Paul VI offered him the presidency of the International Commission for Justice and Peace, but he declined as it would mean excessive absence from his diocese.

One event showed the Pope's high esteem for the Polish prelate's spirituality. In 1976 Cardinal Wojtyla was invited to preach the retreat to the papal household. He took particular care with the lectures which were delivered in Italian; they have been issued as a book, *Sign of Contradiction*. On another occasion Paul VI manifested his support of the Archbishop of Cracow. He would have done so presumably no matter who occupied the See, but it was Karol Wojtyla. A head-on clash between the Polish people and the regime was the setting. Nowa Huta, an industrial town in the suburbs of Cracow, its centre the Lenin Steelworks, was to be the first godless urban settlement in the history of Poland. After protests, permission to build a church was grudgingly conceded. Then it was withdrawn. More public protests, those involved brutally harassed by the police. Capitulation by the regime. The workers allegedly bound to their marxist rulers, chose God in splendid defiance.

One day in the month of May, 1977, Cardinal Wojtyla consecrated the building, which was a miracle by its existence. Every sort of mean delaying tactic by the local minions of the regime had failed to arrest the work, much of it voluntary. Among the many messages of congratulation was one from Paul VI. He had sent stone from St Peter's tomb to be placed in the foundation, and some of the lunar rock which the American astronauts had presented to him. He donated the Carrara marble altar. Within a year and a half the man who that day preached before 50,000 people, would be his successor on the throne of Peter.

His successor would benefit by his mode of government. John Paul II, notably in the use of the Synod, has followed the example of Paul VI. He had been one of his staunch supporters in the doctrinal crisis of his pontificate (see article *Humanae Vitae*).

Poland

Poland attained its independence after the first world war. Its territory had been partitioned between Prussia, Russia and Austria. Its sense of national identity was never lost or lessened, in large part due to the strong Catholic faith. Poles and those with deep attachment to them have a sense of destiny in regard to the country, what Hilaire Belloc called the "sacred flame" that abides in the land. Their resilience was never more evident than at the end of the second world war.

John Paul II was nineteen years of age when the war broke out. He lived through the years of German occupation which was followed by the period of stalinist oppression. The Poles were fortunate to have in that phase of their history a spiritual leader of great wisdom and strength, Cardinal Wzyshinski. He suffered the fate of the other national primates, Stepinac, Beran, Mindszenty in the worst years - internment; there was no torture or ill-treatment in his case. National support for him was manifested in a moment of total splendour through the years of darkness. On 26 August, feast of Our Lady of Czestochowa, 1956, one million people assembled at the shrine on Jasna Gora. They had travelled from all over Poland, with any and every form of makeshift transport. High above the mighty throng, which even hardened foreign journalists looked on with awe, was an empty chair, decked in red and white roses, the national colours. Everyone knew who should have been there.

Soon after, the crisis following Khruschev's denunciation of Stalin broke. The new government, headed by Gomulka, needed the Cardinal's stabilising influence. He was released. His first words are often quoted: "Poles have shown that they can die for Poland; now they must show that they can live for her." He was there at the helm spiritually for a decade. Then the communists thought they could dispense with him. In the Millennium year, 1966, a campaign was launched against him on the state controlled media, press, radio, television. The pretext was that in sending an invitation to the German bishops to attend the planned church ceremonies, he was unpardonably oblivious of the enmity of Germans towards his country. It was a gesture of Christian forgiveness, made without attenuating the facts of history (see article *World War Two*); and the Cardinal acted in concert with all the Polish bishops.

He was the principal target because he was the towering giant; the government feared that through his personality and worldwide prestige the Church would dwarf their part in the Millennium celebration. They did their best to sabotage this event, refusing visas to foreign groups, even eventually to the Pope. They were persistently unjust, and in one instance pathetically petty; they refused the Cardinal's request for a visa needed to travel to Rome for an important ceremony.

The other bishops who were to leave with him remained in the country as a sign of solidarity. The Hierarchy as a whole, led by the Archbishop of Cracow, published a letter strongly supporting him, lauding his truly patriotic spirit. His personal response was dignified and noble. On Holy Thursday night he spoke words which will live forever: "I shall, in the Mandatum ceremony, wash the feet of the old men you see at the end of the church; tonight I would wash the feet of anyone in the world, even of those who think me their enemy." In his Easter Sunday homily he recalled a wartime incident. He was walking through the city at night, it was Easter, and a man accosted him, with the words: "Priest of God, Christ is risen and Poland will rise."

The Cardinal lived to see unexpected change. As he had seen Warsaw restored to its former power from the mass of ruins left by the retreating army, so he saw Gomulka fade from office and Edward Gierek, a conciliatory figure, take his place. Tension between Church and State was eased. One factor favouring stability was the solidarity of the bishops. There were moments when the regime thought that they might divide Wojtyla, their favourite, from Wzyshinski the intransigent one. A lost cause from the first word. Moreover the lion of Warsaw knew just how far to go, without compromise. He was often asked for lessons on how to deal with communists in power. He thought every situation was singular not allowing general rules. He had one mighty advantage. The Poles were united and they seemed to have had the intuition that you cannot put the whole town in jail.

The large-scale change did not come until the triumph of the Solidarity movement, which was after the election of John Paul II. But things were moving that way and his visit to the homeland in the year after his election, spurred those seeking a new Poland. That the country in freedom, shared now with other eastern European countries, has shown unexpected political developments is a puzzle which is for future solution. The reference is to the recent elections and some political controversy over the Concordat first since that signed in 1925.

It is of interest to note the opening clauses of the first Concordat between the Vatican and Poland since 1925. I quote them here below:

This is the first concordat between the Vatican and the Republic of Poland since 1925 (that agreed in 1925 was abrogated by the communists). Two copies, one in Italian and the other in Polish, were signed at Warsaw on 28 July, 1993. Monsignor Joséf Kowalczyk signed for the Holy See, and His Excellency Krzysztof Skubiszewski, Minister of Foreign Affairs, for the Republic of Poland.

The Holy See and the Republic of Poland
- in the intent to regulate, in a stable and harmonious fashion, mutual relations;
- keeping in mind that the Catholic religion is practised by most Polish citizens;
- considering the Catholic Church's mission, the role that the Church has played the thousand-year history of the Polish State, and the meaning of the pontificate of His Holiness John Paul II for Poland's contemporary history;
- considering the decisive importance of the reconquering of independence and sovereignty for the Polish State, and caring about its development;
- noticing the considerable contribution of the Church to the development of the human being and the strengthening of morality;
- guided by the aforesaid values, by the common principles of International Law, by the principles concerning respect for human rights and fundamental freedoms, and by the elimination of all forms of intolerance and discrimination against religion;
- considering that the development of a free and democratic society is founded on the respect of a human being's dignity and rights;
- acknowledging the new organizational structure of the Church in Poland, decreed by the Pontifical Bull "Totus Tuus Poloniae populus";
- the Republic of Poland, having taken into consideration its constitutional principles and its laws, and the Holy See, the documents of Vatican Council II

regarding religious freedom and the relations between the Church and the political community, as well as the norms of canon law, have decided to stipulate the following Concordat.

Therefore, the Holy See, represented by His Excellency Monsignor Joséf Kowalczyk, Appointed Archbishop of Eraclea and Apostolic Nuncio in Warsaw, and the Republic of Poland, represented by His Excellency Mr Krzysztof Skubiszewski, Minister of Foreign Affairs, have established, in mutual agreement, the following:

Article 1
The Republic of Poland and the Holy See reaffirm that the State and the Catholic Church are, each in its individual order, independent and autonomous, and pledge the full respect of this principle in their reciprocal relations and their collaboration for the promotion of man and the common good.

Article 2
In order to maintain and strengthen relations between the contracting parties and to complete the mission assigned to them, an Apostolic Nuncio shall reside, henceforth, in the Polish capital, and an extraordinary and plenipotentiary Ambassador of Poland to the Holy See shall reside in Rome.

Article 3
The Republic of Poland guarantees to the Catholic Church, and to its judicial and constitutional people, the freedom of contact and communication with the Holy See, with the Episcopal Conference, with particular churches, but also with other communities, institutions, organizations, and people, within the country as well as outside Poland.

Press, The

The Press and the Pope is an intriguing subject, too vast to permit of generalizations without serious, prolonged research. He has not given many interviews; one recently to a journalist of *La Stampa* was given wide publicity. The Catholic press has not been uniformly supportive of him, whereas the secular press has seen, at times, the value of his initiatives and his teaching.

Evidently some Catholic papers are the products of extremists of the left and of the right. Some are entirely limited in their outlook by concentration on European countries. They fail to see that the policy of a Pope has to be universal, embracing all cultures and peoples of the world. If they criticize the Pope for travelling so much, it may be their objection to see him travel outside Europe.

An ideological press tends, at times, by its nature, to see what is happening as a sign of approval for its theses - if it is getting what it wants. But what happens is not necessarily good. It may be very bad. The fact that abortion is widely legal at the present time is not a sign of progress. It is a symptom of a dying civilization, of abandonment of moral values, of acceptance of a fallacy which panders to human weakness. The "right to choice" which is the slogan of those favouring abortion is inherently erroneous. The right to choice has no meaning until the area of lawful choice is fixed. Terrorists act on the assumption that they have a right to choice where the lives of others are involved. Burglars act on the idea that the property of others falls within their right to choice. The life of another, whether in the womb or outside it, is not within the lawful area of any one else's choice. It is sacred.

One frequent dodge of journalists who criticize the Pope is retreat into the future. We saw a good deal of this in comments on the Encyclical *Veritatis Splendor*. Journalists told us with an air of near infallibility, how the future would react to the document. What do they know about the future? Nothing more than anyone else. The bishop who condemned Joan of Arc to be burned as a witch, and all the theologians who supported him, scarcely foresaw the verdict that later would vindicate her and disgrace them.

The greatest theologian of the present century, also a staunch supporter of John Paul II, was not appreciated in his lifetime. He was not invited to Vatican II where some of the experts would not count beside him, Hans Urs von Balthasar.

There are Catholic reviews and papers which recognise the Pope's greatness and, on at least one occasion, a widely distributed Brazil daily featured a Public Opinion poll on the question: Who is the person you most admire? Result, John Paul - number one. A brilliant journalist on the French *Figaro*, André Frossard, author of *Dieu existe: je l'ai rencontré*, is an unashamed admirer of the Pope; he collaborated with him on one book, *N'ayez pas peur*, wrote another about him, *Portrait de Jean Paul II*.

Catholic papers are on the whole, not entirely, fair or impartial to the Pope. The one paper to obtain for accurate information, with the texts of most addresses and writings is *L'Osservatore Romano*, of which a weekly selection is issued in many languages. There are reviews and magazines of the highest quality committed to the Pope: *Inside the Vatican*, *The Catholic World Report*, *Trenta Ciorni*, *Catholic International*, *Christ to the World*, *Faith*, and among theological reviews the excellent *Communio*; the official bulletin of the American Fellowship of Catholic scholars is also reliable and informative.

Priests

John Paul II found the crisis in the Catholic priesthood a real, disturbing element in the life of the Church. It is said that hundreds of applications for dispensation from priestly vows were on his desk as soon as he reached it. He refused to grant them until he had assurance that everything possible had been done to help the applicants. He set about strengthening the faith and raising the morale of priests. On Holy Thursday he frequently celebrated a day of the priesthood, with large numbers of priests joining him in the liturgical ceremony. For Holy Thursday in most years of his pontificate he addressed a special letter to the priests of the Church, singling out each year some topic relevant to their office and to the contemporary situation. When possible, in the course of his travels, he ordained candidates to the sacerdotal ministry, setting out the idealism of their calling in the appropriate homily. Again and again in addresses to priestly gatherings in Rome, for example in meetings with the General Chapters of orders or religious congregations of priests, he spoke in similar terms. In the Apostolic Exhortation *Pastores dabo vobis* he put emphasis on the ideals which should be at the core of training for the high office and its practice. John Paul II, from his first Encyclical has emphasized the magnificent, beneficial mystery of the Eucharist (qv) with which, in his thinking, on the lines of the Church's tradition, is intrinsically linked to the priesthood of Christ shared with his ordained ministers. Priesthood was the subject of his weekly catechesis in 1993.

The Pope has shown his concern for a tendency in the ranks of the clergy to obliterate in conduct, occupation, life-style the differences between priests and laity. In March, 1994 a hundred page manual was issued with his formal approval to show priests what they must not do at the present time. They must wear clothes which identify them as priests. They must avoid affectation or luxury in their living quarters, means of transport and choice of holidays.

The Church adheres to its rule of clerical celibacy - on this subject Paul VI issued an Encyclical. Priests are given specific advice on how they must protect their celibacy.

Priests are reminded that they must not actively participate in politics save in extraordinary circumstances and with permission from Rome. They are warned against the assumption that the Church is a democracy; it is a hierarchical organisation. Akin to this principle is the rejection of dissent publicly expressed in regard to Church teachings on faith and morals. This is a grave matter, as it produces scandal and confusion among the faithful.

Dissent is a subject of deep concern to anyone who respects the unity of the Church. It was dealt with at length in the *Instruction on the Ecclesial Vocation of the Theologian*, drawn up by the Congregation for the Doctrine of the Faith (cf article *Ratzinger, Joseph Cardinal*). It is relevant to the life of priests, since most theologians with status in the Church are priests and all priests are trained by them. In the *Instruction* we read: "Dissent is generally defended by various arguments, two of which are more basic in character. The first lies in the order of hermeneutics. The documents of the Magisterium, it is said, reflect nothing more than a debatable theology. The second takes theological pluralism sometimes to a point of relativism which calls the integrity of the faith into question. Here the interventions of the Magisterium would have their origin in one theology among many theologies, while no particular theology, however, could claim universal normative status. In opposition to and in competition with the authentic magisterium, there thus arises a kind of 'parallel magisterium' of theologians.

> Certainly it is one of the theologians's tasks to give a correct interpretation of the Magisterium, and to this end he employs various hermeneutical rules. Among these is the principle which affirms that Magisterial teaching, by virtue of divine assistance, had a validity beyond it argumentation, which may derive at times from a particular theology. As far as theological pluralism is concerned, this is only legitimate to the extent that the unity of faith in its objective meaning is not jeopardized. Essential bonds link the distinct levels of unity of faith, unity-plurality of expressions of the faith, and plurality of theologies. The ultimate reason for plurality is found in the unfathomable mystery of Christ, who transcends every objective systematization. This cannot mean that it is possible to accept conclusions contrary to the mystery and it certainly does not put into question the truth of those assertions by which the Magisterium has declared itself. As to the 'parallel magisterium', it can cause great spiritual harm by opposing its influence to the point of shaping a common opinion, it tends to become the rule of conduct. This cannot but seriously trouble the People of God and lead to contempt for true authority.

The Instruction from which these words are quoted was approved by John Paul II, who ordered its publication. It bears the signature of Cardinal Ratzinger, Prefect and of Mgr A Bovone, Secretary of the Congregation, 24 March, 1990.

Ratzinger, Joseph Cardinal (b. 1927)

Though slightly impaired in health quite recently, this German theologian, heading the Congregation for the Doctrine of the Faith over the last eleven years, has been a powerful ally of John Paul II. Known already during Vatican II as a true expert in his field he went on to teach with brilliance in Munich before becoming Archbishop of Munich, eventually nominated to his present post. No one of his predecessors in that office is comparable with him in expertise and articulate expression: a born communicator in an area where this skill is most valuable. As John Paul II was trained in philosophy, Ratzinger was in theology. Therefore his advice has been to the Pope complementary. When Bishop von Schönborn, OP was asked who were the important theologians in an age which came after one of gold, the forties and fifties of the present century, he singled out the Pope and Ratzinger. Many of his publications will not be available to the general public in English; his *Introduction to Christianity* will whet the appetite for more. *The Ratzinger Report* is widely distributed. It is a book composed on the basis of conversations with a journalist in 1984. It is one of the best analyses of the present mentality, and lack of mentality, in the Church in the post-conciliar period.

In 1972 Ratzinger with Henri (later Cardinal) de Lubac and Hans Urs von Balthasar, both prestigious names, founded the review *Communio*, a response to *Concilium*, the organ of progressive theologians. It now circulates in thirteen languages, maintains a singularly high standard. Ratzinger is not content with watching current publications. He keeps up a constant flow of original essays in theology. The one on the *Church as communion* issued in 1992 was highly significant.

Cardinal Ratzinger has been honoured by the French Academy of Moral and Political Sciences by election to that body. *Time* magazine submitted, by mutual agreement, a number of searching questions to him on the present state of the Church. His replies were not published in full; they appear in *The Catholic World Report*, January 1994 pp.22-31.

Russia

After the consolidation of the Communist regime in Russia the country became a matter of world concern. The tentacles of its tyranny spread everywhere under the direction of the most ruthless ruler the world has ever known. The instruments of his power, foremost among them the KGB, were lethally efficient; his victims were counted in millions. His perverse economic theory was rigidly imposed and was pitifully lauded by qualified people abroad; his influence ramified through communist parties and "fellow-travellers." He gathered the fruits of world war two by dictating his peace terms to Churchill, Roosevelt and Truman. His agents induced top scientists to deliver to him the secret of the hydrogen bomb, and much else that would be classified. Writers and artists within Russia were intellectually enslaved or in prison - at one artistic exhibition some time before his death over eighty per ent of the entries were related to him personally.

How would the Russian people be freed of this monster? A pre-war illusion was crushed by the event: in a war when the people had weapons in their hands they would rise against the tyrant. They fought with unexampled courage and endurance for Mother Russia: the stockades still show where the German invader had reached before Moscow, which did not surrender. Nor did Leningrad, besieged for 900 days, with a million dead. All were united against the enemy not against their own regime; they brought down Hitler's power at Stalingrad.

Stalin retained power. The system he had erected seemed impregnable. The year 1956 three years after his death offered a glimmer of hope. Khruschev denounced the tyrant at the twentieth party congress. The Russian hegemony seemed about to crumble. A change of rulers in Warsaw loosened the dependence on Moscow (see article *Poland*), but the Hungarians went too far and their rising was crushed by the Russian tanks.

All the time the prayers were ascending to God from Catholics attentive to the message of Fatima (qv). Clearly a change in the regime would be a preliminary, if not a condition, of a religious revival. An atmosphere of freedom was needed for a full flowering of the religion which Russia had lived for centuries, which had been driven underground. That seemed a remote possibility. But then occurred the surprising events during the years of Mikhail Gorbachev's tenure of the highest office; *Glasnost* and *Perestroika* eventually led to a loosening of the iron-clad political structure. In the subsequent vicissitudes, which do not concern us Gorbachev himself was deprived of his office, but not before he had taken some utterly unforeseen initiatives.

On 29 April, 1988 in the Catherine Hall in the Kremlin, the Patriarch and five Metropolitans met Gorbachev. The Russian leader began by admitting the mistakes of the past, acknowledged the support given by believers to *Perestroika* and promised a new law on freedom of conscience. "Believers" he said "are Soviet people, workers, patriots, and they have the full right to express their convictions with dignity."

On 1 December 1989 the mega-event of the century took place. Gorbachev met John Paul II in the Vatican. In his address the Pope said:

> Your visit enables us to look with greater confidence to the future of the communities of believers in the Soviet Union... and the law on freedom of conscience, soon to be discussed by the Supreme Soviet, will help to guarantee to all believers the full exercise of the right to religious freedom which, as I have said many times, is the foundation of the other freedoms.

Gorbachev spoke of the meeting as a "truly extraordinary event." "We had much to discuss." He continued:

> I feel that my thoughts and concerns have been duly appreciated, as well as my explanations of the problems that now exist in our country, including problems between the state and various churches, which we are addressing in a spirit of democracy and humanism and within the framework of *Perestroika*.. People of

many confessions, including Christians, Moslems, Jews, Buddhists and others
live in the Soviet Union. All of them have a right to satisfy their spiritual needs.
Shortly a Law on the Freedom of Conscience will be adopted in our country.

Could anyone anticipate that the successor in office of Stalin would visit the Pope in
Rome, invite him to come to Russia, offer diplomatic relations with the Vatican -
which were established on 15 March, 1990, and promise a charter of religious
freedom, which has been legally enacted, though there are remaining points of
contention? The word miracle has been used in commentaries on this sequence of
events.

This brings us to the vexed problem of Fatima, the consecration to the Immaculate
Heart of Mary, and the conversion of Russia. Our Lady had told the children at
Fatima that she would come to ask for the consecration of Russia to her Immaculate
Heart to avert a world war. In 1929 the request became formal to the survivor of
the visionaries, now a nun in Spain, Sister Lucia. It was transmitted to Rome, but
nothing was done. In 1942 Pius XII made the consecration of the world, with an
oblique reference to Russia; in 1952, in his Encyclical, *Sacro Vergente Anno* he
made the consecration of Russia: the Encyclical was addrssed to the Russian people.
Paul VI associated himself with this act in his discourse closing the third session of
Vatican II, where the Marian chapter of the Constitution on the Church had been
passed; that day also he had proclaimed Mary Mother of the Church.

John Paul II was informed more fully on Fatima (qv) after the assassination attempt
than he had been previously; literature was read to him by a friend while he was in
hospital. He knew then of Our Lady's request for the consecration of Russia to her
Immaculate Heart. Has he made the consecration as she wished it? There are
pockets, not very small, of acrimonious criticism on the point, one based in North
America, the other in France. There were two conditions sought: the consecration
should be made by the Pope in conjunction with all the bishops of the Church, on a
fixed day. Has John Paul II done this? In Fatima for the anniversary of his
preservation from death, 13 May 1982, he delivered a homily in which he spoke
lengthily of the meaning of consecration to the Immaculate Heart of Mary; he
recalled the consecration of the world and of Russia by Pius XII. He spoke these
words:

> My heart is oppressed when I see the sin of the world and the whole range of menaces
> gathering like a dark cloud over mankind, but it also rejoices with hope as I once
> more do what has been done by my predecessors, when they consecrated the world
> to the Heart of the Mother, when they consecrated especially to that Heart those
> peoples which particularly need to be consecrated... Once more this act is being
> done. Mary's appeal is not for just once. Her appeal must be taken up by generation
> after generation, in accordance with the ever new 'signs of the times.' It must be
> unceasingly returned to. It must ever be taken up anew.

Was this the proper response to Our Lady's request? Apparently the Pope himself did not think so. On 25 March, 1984 in St Peter's Basilica in Rome, where he had brought the statue of Our Lady from Fatima, he renewed the act of consecration. It was more explicit in terms. More important, it had been preceded by a message sent to the bishops of the entire Church that the Pope intended to make this consecration. Some words may be quoted:

> And therefore, O Mother of individuals and peoples, you who know all their sufferings and their hopes, you who have a mother's awareness of all the struggles between good and evil, between light and darkness, which afflict the modern world, accept the cry which we, moved by the Holy Spirit, address directly to your Heart. Embrace with the Love of the Mother and Handmaid of the Lord, this human world of ours, which we entrust and consecrate to you, for we are full of concern for the earthly and eternal destiny of individuals and peoples.

> In a special way we entrust and consecrate to you those individuals and nations which particularly need to be thus entrusted and consecrated... The power of this consecration lasts for all time and embraces all individuals, peoples and nations.

Was this the definite answer? When the Bishop of Fatima thanked the Pope for consecrating the world to the Immaculate Heart of Mary, John Paul II replied "and Russia." But he did not name Russia. Hence the controversy. Why he did not name Russia is a matter of conjecture. Possibly he thought that the Orthodox would be offended; he probably knew that tension would arise from his appointment of a Catholic Archbishop as Apostolic Administrator of the Latin Catholics of the Republic of Russia with his seat in Moscow.

Was the consecration collegial, that is involving all the Bishops? That depended on each of them personally. The Pope had informed them. But another voice is customarily heard in this debate - if one must use the word, that of the survivor of the 1917 apparitions and of the 1929 message, Sister Lucia, now a Carmelite in the monastery of Coimbra. She is known to have expressed the view that the prayer of the Pope at Fatima in 1982 was not what Our Lady desired. In letters written after the act of 25 March, 1984, she stated that now what Our Lady wanted was done. Here there are two questions to be considered. Were the letters written by her? Does she speak as specially enlightened by Our Lady, or as acting on her own judgement? An answer to the first question is in her own words: "Yes, I wrote these letters... I know the letters that you mean. Some people have gone so far as to say that they are forgeries. Yes, I wrote these letters. No one answers my mail but me." These words were spoken in an interview given by Sister Lucia to Cardinal Padiyara of Ernaculam, India and others on 11 October, 1992. Sister Lucia said much the same next day to Ambassador Howard Dee of the Philippines and Corazon ("Cory") Aquino.

As to the exact source of Sister Lucia's verdict we have no certainty. She has an aura in the Catholic Church, akin to that - for a different reason, of Mother Teresa of Calcutta. But was she giving a judgement of Our Lady? That we cannot say.

Some other incidents a propos the Pope and Russia. His confidant and informant on Russia and Eastern Europe, Bishop Hlnilica, a Czechoslovak, former prisoner for the faith, ordained in clandestine circumstances, was in Moscow on 25 March, 1984. He took an unusual initiative. Behind a copy of *Pravda*, the party daily paper, he actually said Mass within the Church of the Assumption (at the time a museum, now open to worship) inside the Kremlin, and then read the act of consecration of Russia to the Immaculate Heart of Mary; the Pope was deeply moved when he heard of it.

The first televised programme direct from Fatima to Russian screens took place on 13 October, 1991. It was of 75 minutes duration at 12.15 and again in the evening; because of the widespread interest a repeat went out on 7 November, anniversary - by coincidence? - of the 1917 communist revolution.

Jose Correa, Managing Director of the Catholic Radio and Television Network based in Belgium, was in Moscow for different programmes. He had a full radio station with him. At the crisis in the 1991 coup he lent this station to Boris Yeltsin, who used it to make contact with the Russian people, thus defeating the rebels. When Yeltsin asked Correa what he would like by way of thanks he replied "permission to broadcast live from Fatima to Russia." The Russian agreed at once.

The religious revival continues in Russia. One sees religious programmes on television; there is a regular religious radio programme. Churches are crowded and there is widespread interest in Christian iconography. When the International Peace Pilgrimmage, 1992, reached Moscow, its participants could join in the World Catholic Youth Congress held in the Kosmos hotel. For the final ceremony fifty priests and five bishops joined in a concelebrated Mass - some years previously this was impossible. On 16 October the statue of Our Lady of Fatima (which had been borne with a guard of honour from the plane to the terminal) was crowned in Red Square. A dream of St Maximilian Kolbe had been realized.

Quite recently, President Yeltsin has restored two of the most famous icons in the world - Our Lady of Vladimir and Rublev's Trinity, to the Church of the Assumption. Hitherto, they were museum pieces in The Tretirkov. The Church which will house the icon of Our Lady of Thazan is nearing completion.

For further information: Timothy Tindal-Robertson, *Fatima, Russia and Pope John Paul II*, Devon, 1992.

Sapieha, Adam Cardinal (d. 1951)

Of a Polish princely family, with experience of the Roman Curia where he had worked for years, Cardinal Sapieha, Archbishop of Cracow, had his greatest hour in the ordeal of his country during the second world war. He embodied Polish defiance, as Cardinal Mercier had done in Belgium during the first world war, never compromised, emerged finally as one who exemplified the true patriotic, Catholic Polish spirit. He influenced the life of Karol Wojtyla decisively. When the young man made known his wish to become a Carmelite priest the Archbishop suggested that he follow the courses in the clandestine seminary which the Cardinal had organised in Cracow; he could decide later on his future. After Karol's priestly ordination the Cardinal sent him to Rome where he was received in the Belgian seminary; the rector was Mgr Furstenberg, who would later as a Cardinal help to elect him Pope. Cardinal Sapieha encouraged his future successor in the See of Cracow to move about among the Polish diaspora in Europe. It was all part of a providential preparation for a mighty role.

Second World War, The

In 1966, the Polish Millennium year, the hierarchy of the country sent a lengthy letter to the German bishops inviting them to the celebration which was planned. They set forth frankly a summary statement of the Polish experience during the German occupation of their country:

> After a short independence lasting about twenty years (1918-1939) Poland, through no fault of her own, felt crashing upon her what has euphemistically been called the second world war, which by us was considered total annihilation. Our poor country sank into a dark and sinister night such as in generations we had never known. This night all of us called 'the time of the German occupation' and thus it will remain in the history of Poland. We were reduced to helplessness. Our country was covered with concentration camps, in which chimneys from the crematoria smoked day and night. More than six million Polish citizens, in majority Jewish, paid for the occupation with their lives. The Polish intelligentsia was simply swept away; 2,000 priests and five bishops (one quarter of the existing hierarchy) went into concentration camps. Hundreds of priests and tens of thousands of civilians were the victims of summary execution in the first days of the war (278 priests in the diocese of Kulm alone). The diocese of Wloclawek lost 48 per cent of its priests during the war, Kulm 47 per cent. Many others were deported. All secondary and higher schools were closed. Seminaries were suppressed. Every German uniform, not only that of the SS, became for every Pole an object of hatred. There is no Polish family which has not war victims among its members. We do not wish to give every

detail so as not to open wounds which are not yet healed, but if we recall the terrible night through which Poland passed it is solely that our present mentality should be understood...

The Nazi programme was part of Karol Wojtyla's curriculum vitae. Even preaching to the papal household in 1976 he recalled the concentration camps. In those years Polish resilience, which is legendary, was stretched to the limit. It still sufficed. Young people, university students like Karol Wojtyla, had to work and carry an *arbeitskarte* if they were to escape the SS or Gestapo net, and whatever fate a brutal commander would decree. The young Wojtyla went to work in a stone quarry at Zakrzow outside Cracow. Hewing stones in conditions of such misery would scarcely appear inspiring. Yet in later years when the quarry worker had turned to different occupations, it inspired his poetry. One of these poems, "The Stone Quarry," starting from the physical, somewhat repellent details of the daily toil rises to visions of human power, interweaves ideals of human self-mastery with the hard task of conquering stone, speaks of love as a dynamic in life.

The workman rose a degree higher in the labour-force when he changed to the Solway chemical factory in Cracow. He told 2,500 workers gathered in Rome on 9 December, 1978:

> For a short period of my life I too had personal experience of factory work. I know what the task of daily labour means to those dependent on others. I know dullness and monotony. I know the needs of the working class, their just demands and their lawful aspirations. And I know how necessary it is that work should never be a thing to alienate and frustrate, but should match the higher spiritual dignity of man.

Social Teaching

John Paul II has taken every opportunity given him to show the importance of the Church's social teaching, whether in addressing specialist assemblies on subjects like world population, or in issuing with his own authority and composition the findings of the 1980 synod on the family, in *Familiaris Consortio*, 22 November, 1981, or in pleading for human rights in troubled situations; for the Year of the Family he issued a special letter. His incessant, resolute, optimistic campaign on behalf of world and local peace, despite the apparently discouraging facts which he realistically measures, is itself a social commitment of the highest value. To have his explicit, formal, plenary teaching in this domain account must be taken of three Encyclicals, *Laborem Exercens*, 14 September, 1981, for the ninetieth anniversary of Leo XIII's great Encyclical, *Rerum Novarum*; *Sollicitudo Rei Socialis*, 30 December, 1987, for the twentieth anniversary of Paul VI's Encyclical, *Populorum Progressio*; and

Centesimus Annus, for the centenary of *Rerum Novarum*, 1 May, 1991. In each of these important documents John Paul II skillfully singles out the essential enduring points in the texts he is commemorating and relates them to the contemporary situation, adding insights of his own. Thus he alludes respectfully to the changing situation in the Third World countries, noting the evils that have arisen, when he is dealing with *Populorum Progressio*. In his first commemorative Encyclical on *Rerum Novarum* he relates the theology of work to the technological age. In the second he analyses carefully the breakdown in the socialist empire, not forgetting to mention Solidarity in his own country.

As always the Pope is attentive to what Vatican II (qv) has to add to the papal teaching. As always, he concludes each Encyclical with a prayer to Our Lady. It is a fair comment that these papal pronouncements have not been given the attention they deserve. They are the product of a keen intellect, a fully informed memory, experience of social systems, structures, abuses, achievements which for one in his position is unexampled. Taken with his Encyclical on the moral order they constitute a most precious corpus of papal doctrine (see article *Veritatis Splendor*).

Spirit, The Holy

In 1990, the Pope chose as the subject of his annual Holy Thursday Letter to priests the Holy Spirit, this time his approach being, let the Spirit act in us. The reader who may be sceptical about the insistence in the present work on this theme as a dominant one in the Pope's teaching may be reassured by consulting the articles on *Mission* and *Catechetics* and by the following survey of papal utterances on the subject: in the year 1990, *La Documentation Catholique*, a reliable, though not totally complete record of papal statements, showed that there were thirty-six passages in various addresses and writings of the Pope on the subject; in 1991 there were, according to the same publication, twenty-seven passages referring, in more or less detail, to the subject.

Is the Pope himself conscious of what he has been teaching, of the fact that in this matter he is an innovator? Let the reader judge by his words spoken on 12 June, 1984 at the World Council of Churches:

> There is another aspect of the Christian mystery which unites us more than in the past. We have together learned to understand better the entire role of the Holy Spirit. But this *rediscovery* (emphasis added) - which marks the renewal of Catholic liturgy -has rendered us sensitive to new dimensions of our ecclesial life. The Spirit is the source of a liberty in faithfulness that we have received from the generations which have gone before us. He can find new ways when there is question of walking together towards a unity which is, at the same time, based

on truth and yet is respectful of the rich diversity of really Christian values which spring from a common patrimony (cf Decree on Ecumenism, n.4).

From the fact of this new attention to the presence of the Spirit our prayer has taken on a special accent. It is more fully opened to the action of grace, in which we detach ourselves from our own preoccupations to fix our gaze on the work of God and the wonder of his grace. This gaze enables us to have a more lively consciousness of God's design on his people, with certainty on the primacy of divine initiatives. We are not satisfied with uttering pleas and intercession together; we tend more now to bless God for the work of his grace. Prayer has a special place in our options. Though it is not yet possible to celebrate the Lord's Eucharist together, communicating at the same table, we have it more and more at heart to make prayer in common the centre of our meetings. (DC 1984, 705).

The Pope continues on the same theme. As this article is being typed, 1 April, 1994 one may read in *OR*, 16 March, the text of his catechesis of 9 March, on lay people in the Church. On the Holy Spirit he spoke thus:

However, now we must add that the Holy Spirit, the giver of every gift and the first principle of the Church's vitality, does not only work through the Sacraments. According to St Paul he distributes to each his own gifts as he wills (cf 1 Cor 12:11) pouring out into the People of God a great wealth of graces both for prayer and contemplation and for action. They are *charisms*: lay people receive them too, especially in relation to their mission in the Church and society. The Second Vatican Council stated this in connection with St Paul: 'The Holy Spirit also distributes special graces among the faithful of every rank. By these gifts he makes them fit and ready to undertake various tasks for the renewal and building up of the Church, as it is written (in St Paul) 'the manifestation of the Spirit is given to everyone for profit' (1 Cor 12:7 - *Lumen Gentium*, 12).

St Paul highlighted the multiplicity and variety of charisms in the early Church; some are extraordinary, such as healings, the gift of prophecy or that of tongues; others are simpler, given for the ordinary fulfilment of the tasks assigned in the community (cf 1 Cor 12:7-10).

As a result of Paul's text, charisms are often thought of as *extraordinary gifts*, which primarily marked the beginning of the Church's life. The Second Vatican Council called attention to charisms in their quality as gifts belonging to the *ordinary* life of the Church and not necessarily having an extraordinary or miraculous nature. The Apostolic Exhortation *Christifideles laici* also spoke of charisms as gifts that can be 'exceptional and great or simple and ordinary' (n.24). In addition, it should be kept in mind that the primary or principal aim of many charisms is not the personal sanctification of those who receive them, but the service of others and the Church's welfare. Certainly they also aim at and serve the growth of personal holiness, but in an essentially altruistic and communitarian perspective, which belongs to the Church's organic dimension in that it concerns the growth of Christ's Mystical Body.

As St Paul told us and the Council repeated, these charisms result from the free choice and gift of the Holy Spirit, in whose property (*proprietas*) as the first and substantial *Gift* within Trinitarian life they share. In a special way the Triune God shows his sovereign power in his *gifts*. This power is not subject to any antecedent rule, to any particular discipline or to a plan of interventions established once and for all; according to St Paul he distributes his gifts to each 'as he wills' (1 Cor 12:11). It is an eternal will of love, whose freedom and gratuitousness is revealed in the action carried out by the Holy Spirit-Gift in the economy of salvation. Through this sovereign freedom and gratuitousness, charisms are also given to the laity, as the Church's history shows (cf *Christifideles laici*, n.24).

We cannot but admire the great wealth of gifts bestowed by the Holy Spirit on lay people as members of the Church in our age as well. Each of them has the necessary ability to carry out the tasks to which he is called for the welfare of the Christian people and the world's salvation, if he is open, docile and faithful to the Holy Spirit's action.

However, we must also turn our attention to another aspect of St Paul's teaching and that of the Church, an aspect that applies to every type of ministry and to charisms: their diversity and variety cannot harm unity. 'There are different gifts but the same Spirit; there are different ministries but the same Lord' (1 Cor 12:4-5). Paul asked that these differences be respected because not everyone can expect to carry out the same role contrary to God's plan and the Spirit's gift, and contrary to the most elementary laws of any social structure. However the Apostle equally stressed the need for unity, which itself answers a sociological demand, but which in the Christian community should even more be a reflection of the divine unity. *One Spirit, one Lord*. Thus, *one Church*.

At the beginning of the Christian era extraordinary things were accomplished under the influence of charisms, both the extraordinary ones and those which could be called little, humble, everyday charisms. This has always been the case in the Church and is so in our era as well, generally in a hidden way, but sometimes in a striking way, when God desires it for the good of his Church. In our day, as in the past, a great number of lay people have contributed to the Church's spiritual and pastoral growth. We can say that there are many people who, because of their charisms, work as good, genuine witnesses of faith and love. It is to be hoped that all will reflect on the transcendent value of eternal life already present in their work, if it is carried out in fidelity to their vocation and with docility to the Holy Spirit who lives and acts in their hearts.

(See articles *Apparitions* and *Vassula Rydén*).

The Pope's teaching on the Holy Spirit is contained primarily in his Encyclical Letter, *Dominum et Vivificantem* (qv). The full corpus, however, comprises a number of other papal pronouncements.[1] The sixteen hundredth anniversary of the Council of Constantinople (qv), 1981 stirred him to different initiatives. On 25 March 1981, he sent a letter to the bishops of the Catholic Church, *A Concilio Constantinopolitano I*, recalling the great themes of the Council's creed and announcing the ceremonies to be held in commemoration of it; twinned with these would be ceremonies to celebrate the fifteen hundred and fiftieth anniversary of the Council of Ephesus, where Mary's divine motherhood was proclaimed. On Pentecost Sunday, 7 June the morning ceremony in St Peter's would recall Constantinople; the late evening gathering in St Mary Major would evoke Ephesus. Between the publication of the letter and the ceremonies planned an attempt was made on the life of the Pope, 13 May 1981. "In this anniversary," wrote the Pope:

we not only call to mind a formula of faith that has been in force for sixteen centuries in the Church; at the same time we make ever more present to our spirit, in reflection, in prayer, in the contribution of spirituality and theology, that personal divine which gives life, that hypostatic Gift - *Dominum et vivificantem* - that Third Person of the most Holy Trinity who in this faith is shared in by each individual soul and by the whole Church. The Holy Spirit continues to vivify the Church and to guide her along the paths to holiness and love.[2]

Dealing with the Council of Ephesus the Pope says:

These two anniversaries, though for different reasons and with differing historical relevance, redound to the honour of the Holy Spirit. All was accomplished *by the power of the Holy Spirit....* The two phrases in the Niceno-Constantinopolitan Creed, 'Et *incarnatus est* de Spiritu Sancto' and 'Credo in Spiritum Sanctum Dominum *et vivificantem*,' remind us that the greatest *work* of the Holy Spirit, one to which all the others unceasingly refer as a source from which they draw, is that of *the incarnation of the Eternal Word* by the power of the Spirit from the Virgin Mary.[3]

---

[1]While awaiting a monograph, recourse must be had to individual texts in AAS, OR, Insegnamenti.
[2]Full text A Concilio Constantinopolitano I, AAS 73 (1981), 513-537; passage quoted, 514.
[3]Ibid, 518, 522.

The Pope develops these ideas, showing how Mary's maternal link with the Church is part of the whole plan.

The Pope has occasionally spoken of the Spirit in the Wednesday audiences to which he willingly gives a catechetical orientation. On 3 August 1983 his theme was the Holy Spirit as the law of humankind redeemed. "What" he asks:

> is the meaning of 'the law of man redeemed is the Holy Spirit?' It means that in the 'new creature' the fruit of Redemption, the Spirit has taken up his abode, realizing a presence of God much more intimate than that following upon the act of creation.

There follows a searching analysis of human personality under the influence of the Spirit which the Pope concludes thus:

> This then is the definition of the ethos of the Redemption and of liberty; it is the ethos which has its origin in the gift of the Spirit who dwells in us; it is the liberty of him who does what he *likes* by doing what he *ought*.[1]

In the Wednesday of Whit week that year the Pope had also spoken of the great work of reconciliation with Christ and with God, of which Pentecost was the prototype.[2]

In the autumn of 1985 John Paul II devoted the Wednesday audiences to a catechesis on the articles of the Creed. On 13 and 20 November he commented on the articles which profess faith in the Holy Spirit. He delayed particularly on the *Filioque* (qv). Recalling the Scripture texts which call the Spirit of the Father, Spirit of the Son and Spirit of Jesus he went on:

> Therefore the Latin Church professes that the Holy Spirit proceeds from the Father and the Son (*qui a Patre Filioque procedit*) while the Orthodox Churches profess that the Holy Spirit proceeds from the Father through the Son. He proceeds 'by way of will,' 'in the manner of love' (*per modum amoris*). This is a *sententia certa*, that is, a theological doctrine commonly accepted in the Church's teaching and therefore sure and binding.

The Pope then gives a lengthy explanation of the spiration, origin of the Holy Spirit. He quotes from the Athanasian Creed, recalls the names the Fathers gave to the third Person:

> It can be said that God in his innermost life is 'love' which is personalized in the

---

[1] OR 4 August 1983.
[2] OR 26 May 1983.

Holy Spirit, the Spirit of the Father and the Son. The Spirit is also called *Gift*. In the Spirit in fact who is Love there is the source of every gift having its origin in God in regard to creatures: the gift of existence by means of creation, the gift of grace through the economy of salvation.[1]

The *Atti del Congresso* reproduce the text of John Paul's address to the members, 26 March, 1982. He rejoiced in the ecumenical character of the gathering and hoped for much from the combined work of the experts:

> For our Church is the Church of the Spirit. And faith in the Holy Spirit is at the heart of our Christian faith, as the creed of the holy Councils professes. It is the Holy Spirit who is at the heart of the sanctification of Christ's disciples. It is he who gives life to their missionary zeal and to their ecumenical prayer. The Spirit it is who is the source and moving power of the renewal of the Church of Christ.[2]

The Pope lauded the work of the theologians, pointing to the need there was for genuine theology to counteract "too many popular works, superficial, insufficiently based, of a kind that could disturb the faith of the Christian people, the faith of the holy Councils."[3]   Interspersed with such practical remarks are briefly phrased insights:

> the Holy Spirit is mysteriously present in the non-Christian religions and cultures. And that also you have sought to articulate... Of the Holy Spirit it can also be said: each one has part of him and all have him wholly, so inexhaustible is his generosity. In the experience of the Churches he is the invisible ferment, recognisable in his fruits as St Paul helps us to discern them in the spiritual life of Christians: in their prayer which regains its sense of praise and gratitude, as well as its confident boldness; in the living communities full of joy and charity, which the Holy Spirit raises up and transfigures; in the spirit of sacrifice; in courageous apostolate and fraternal action in the service of justice and peace. In all the Holy Spirit stimulates the quest for the meaning of life, the obstinate pursuit of beauty, of the good beyond evil... The Holy Spirit acts in persons, in the simplest as in those highly placed - and in communities, beginning with the little domestic churches, families.[4]

The Pope took note of the reawakening of devotion to the Holy Spirit, which called for sound theology; he spoke with great confidence and insistence of the "special

---

[1] OR 21 November 1985.
[2] Atti del Congresso, II, 1515.
[3] Ibid, 1518.
[4] Ibid, 1519, 1520.

grace which we hope for from the Holy Spirit," the realization of Christian unity; and he spoke with feeling of his own personal devotion to the Holy Spirit.

Pope John Paul has had other occasions to express his thoughts on the Holy Spirit, in an address to young people whom he had confirmed on 9 June 1985, in a message for World Mission Day, on 20 October 1985. Noteworthy is the passage on Charisms (qv) in the Apostolic Exhortation, *Christifideles Laici*, 30 December 1988:

The Holy Spirit, while bestowing diverse ministries in Church communion, enriches it still further with particular gifts or promptings of grace called *charisms*. These can take a great variety of forms, both as a manifestation of the absolute freedom of the Spirit who abundantly supplies them, and as a response to the varied needs of the Church in history. The description and the classification given to these gifts in the New Testament are an indication of their rich variety.

The Pope then quotes 1 Cor 12:7-10 and refers to 1 Cor 12:4-6, 28-31; Rom 12:6-8; 1 Pt 4:10-11. He continues:

Whether they be exceptional and great or simple and ordinary, the charisms are graces of the Holy Spirit that have, directly or indirectly, a usefulness for the ecclesial community, ordered as they are to the building up of the Church, to the well-being of humanity and to the needs of the world.

Even in our own time there is no lack of a fruitful manifestation of various charisms among the faithful, women and men. These charisms are given to individual persons, and can even be shared by others in such ways as to continue in time a precious and effective heritage, serving as a source of a particular spiritual affinity among persons. In referring to the apostolate of the lay faithful the Second Vatican Council writes... (here follows the passage from the Decree on the Lay Apostolate, art.3).

By a logic which looks to the divine source of this giving, as the Council recalls,[1] the gifts of the Spirit demand that those who have received them exercise them for the growth of the whole Church.

The charisms are received in gratitude both on the part of the one who receives them, and also on the part of the entire Church. They are in fact a singularly rich source of grace for the vitality of the apostolate and for the holiness of the whole Body of Christ provided that they be gifts that come truly from the Spirit and are exercised in full conformity with the authentic promptings of the Spirit.

---

[1] Footnote quotes the same article of the Decree on the Lay Apostolate.

In this sense the discernment of charisms is always necessary. Indeed the Synod
Fathers have stated: 'The action of the Holy Spirit, who breathes where he will,
is not always easily recognized and received. We know that God acts in all
Christians, and we are aware of the benefits which flow from charisms both for
individuals and for the whole Christian community. Nevertheless, at the same
time we are also aware of the power of sin and how it can disturb and confuse
the life of the faithful and of the community.'

For this reason no charism dispenses a person from reference and submission to
the Pastors of the Church. (There follows a quotation from the Constitution on
the Church, art.12.)[1]

Spirit, The Holy and Jesus

The relationship between the Spirit of Jesus has been brought into focus in recent
theological writings, notably by Y M J Congar, OP.[2] It is a theme taken up with
remarkable insights by John Paul II in the course of the catechetical series which he
has devoted to the Holy Spirit in recent times. Some lengthy passages will represent
not only the Pope's thinking, but very recent theological progress:

Jesus himself illustrates the role of the Spirit when he explains to the disciples
that only with the Spirit's help will they be able to penetrate the depths of the
mystery of his person and mission. 'When the Spirit of truth comes, the Spirit
will guide you into all the truth' (Jn 16:13-14). Therefore, it is the Holy Spirit
who lets people grasp the greatness of Christ and thus 'glorifies' the Saviour.
But it is also the same Spirit who reveals his role in Jesus' life and mission.

This is a point of great interest, to which I wish to direct your attention with this
new series of religious instruction.

If previously we have shown the wonders of the Holy Spirit announced by Jesus
and experienced at Pentecost and during the initial journey of the Church in
history, the time has come to emphasize the fact that the first and greatest wonder
accomplished by the Holy Spirit is Christ himself. It is towards this wonder that
we want to direct your attention.

In fact we have already reflected on the person, life and mission of Christ in the

---

[1]Christifideles Laici, 25, tr. Veritas, Dublin, p. 64-67.
[2]Cf. with bibl. in Veni Creator Spiritus, 46, J D G Dunn, Jesus and the Spirit,
London, 1875; Christ and Spirit in the New Testament: Studies in Honor of C F D
Moule, eds, B Lindars and S S Smalley, Cambridge, 1973.

Christological series: but now we can return briefly to that topic under the heading of pneumatology, that is in the light of the action accomplished by the Holy Spirit within the Son of God made man.

Treating of the topic of the 'Son of God' in catechetical instruction one speaks about him after having considered 'God the Father' and before speaking of the Holy Spirit, who 'proceeds from the Father and the Son.' For this reason Christology precedes pneumatology. And it is right that it is so, because even seen from a chronological standpoint, Christ's revelation in our world happened before the outpouring of the Holy Spirit who formed the Church on the day of Pentecost. Furthermore, that outpouring was the fruit of Christ's redemptive offering and the manifestation of the power acquired by the Son now seated at the Father's right hand.

Still a pneumatological integration with Christology seems to be inevitable - as the Orientals observe - by the fact that the Holy Spirit is found at the very origin of Christ as Word Incarnate come into the world 'by the power of the Holy Spirit,' as the Creed says.

In accomplishing the mystery of the Incarnation, there was a decisive presence of the Spirit, to the degree that, if we want to grasp and enunciate this mystery more fully, it is not enough for us to say that the Word was made flesh; we must also underline -as happens in the Creed - the Spirit's role in forming the humanity of the Son of God in the virginal womb of Mary. We will speak about this later. And we will attempt to follow the Holy Spirit in the life and mission of Christ: in his childhood, in the inauguration of his public life through his Baptism, in his sojourn in the desert, in prayer, in preaching, in sacrifice, and finally, in resurrection.

A basic truth emerged from examination of the Gospel texts: what Christ was, and what he is for us, cannot be understood apart from the Holy Spirit. That means that not only is the Holy Spirit's light necessary for penetrating Christ's mystery, but the influence of the Holy Spirit in the Incarnation of the Word and in the entire life of Christ must be taken into account to explain the Jesus of the Gospel. The Holy Spirit left the mark of his own personality on the face of Christ.

Therefore, arriving at a deeper awareness of Christ demands also a deeper awareness of the Holy Spirit. 'To know who Christ is' and 'to know who the Spirit is' are two indissoulubly linked requirements, the one implying the other.

We can add that even the Christian's relationship with Christ is integrally joined to his or her relationship with the Spirit. The Letter to the Ephesians helps us to understand this when it expressed the hope that believers may be 'strengthened

with power' by the Spirit of the Father in the inner man, in order to be able to
'know Christ's love which surpasses knowledge' (cf. Eph 3:16-19). That means
that in order to reach Christ with our knowledge and love - as happens in true
Christian wisdom - we need the inspiration and the guidance of the Holy Spirit,
the interior master of truth and life.[1]

To this splendid statement of the theological reality here under consideration we may
perhaps add another passage from the teaching of John Paul II; he is speaking of the
holiness of Jesus:

The union of divinity and humanity in the one Person of the Word-Son, that is
the 'hypostatic union' (hypostasis: 'person') is the Holy Spirit's greatest
accomplishment in the history of creation and in salvation history. Even though
the entire Trinity is its cause, still it is attributed by the Gospel and by the
Fathers to the Holy Spirit, because it is the highest work wrought by divine
Love, wrought with the absolute gratuitousness of grace, in order to communicate
to humanity the fullness of holiness in Christ: all these effects are attributed to
the Holy Spirit (Cf. St Thomas, *Summa Theol.*, III, q.32, a.1).

The words addressed to Mary during the Annunciation indicate that the Holy
Spirit is the source of holiness for the Son who is to be born of her. At the
instant in which the Eternal Word becomes man, a unique fullness of human
holiness is accomplished in the assumed nature, a fullness which goes beyond that
of any other saint, not only of the Old but also of the New Covenant. This
holiness of the Son of God as man, as Son of Mary, a holiness from the source,
rooted in the hypostatic union - is the work of the Holy Spirit, who will continue
to act in Christ to the point of crowning his masterpiece in the Easter mystery.[2]

The Pope goes on to show how this type of holiness is a result of the unique
consecration effected in Christ by the Spirit, how he is the unique exemplar of the
"law of the Spirit" (Rom 8:2), how his "consecration" is made known at the level of
mission at the start of his messianic activity:

'The Spirit of the Lord is upon me: because he has anointed me; he has sent me'
(Lk 4:18). The mystery-reality of the Incarnation, therefore, signals the entrance
into the world of a new holiness. It is the holiness of the divine Person of the
Son-Word who, in hypostatic union with humanity, permeates and consecrates
the entire reality of the Son of Mary: soul and body. By the power of the Holy

[1]General audience, March 28, 1990, L'Osservatore Romano, English ed., April 2, 1990.
[2]General audience, June 6, 1990, L'Osservatore Romano, English ed., June 11, 1990.

Spirit, the holiness of the Son of Man constitutes the principle and lasting source of holiness in human and world history.[1]

The Pope elsewhere reflects on the anthropological dimension of the mystery:

We can say, therefore, that in the Incarnation the Holy Spirit lays the foundations for a new anthropology which sheds light on the greatness of human nature as reflected in Christ. In him, in fact, human nature reaches its highest point of union with God, 'having been conceived by the power of the Holy Spirit in such a way that one and the same subject can be Son of God and son of man' (St Thomas, *Summa Theol.*, III, q.2, a.12, ad 3). It was not possible for man to rise up higher than this high point, nor is it possible for human thought to conceive of a closer union with the divinity.[2]

The Pope's general ideas offer a valid schema wherein the details of the Spirit's intervention in Christ's life can be fully studied. This is done in *Veni Creator Spiritus*.[3]

Spirit, the Holy and Mary, Mother of God

One of the themes to come to prominence in theological discourse since Vatican II is the nature of the relationship between Mary and the Holy Spirit. The great Russian Orthodox theologian Sergius Bulgakov (d.1944) had a very challenging theory on the subject. He spoke of the Holy Spirit making a "hypostatic descent" on the Virgin Mary at the Annunciation; he remained ever after with her in "the full force of the Annunciation." More recently it has been said that Mary personified the Holy Spirit, a term capable of misunderstanding. Since the time of St Francis of Assisi, Mary has been occasionally spoken of as Spouse of the Holy Spirit. St Louis Marie Grignion de Montfort accepted the term enthusiastically, as did his disciple, St Maxmilian Kolbe in our time. Three Popes have also done so, Leo XIII, Pius XII and John Paul II. The Fathers of Vatican II did not use it to designate the sublime relationship; they preferred "sanctuary" of the Holy Spirit, an idea applicable to all Christians.

John Paul II has justified the use he makes of it. In an address on 2 May, 1990, he spoke at length of the bridal aspect of Mary's life with God. First he traces the idea of Israel as the bride of God through the Old Testament. Then he makes the

---

[1] Ibid.
[2] General audience, May 23, 1990, L'Osservatore Romano, English ed., May 28, 1990.
[3] Op. cit., 44-46.

application to Mary:

> These extraordinary texts of the Old Testament prophets find their true fulfilment in the mystery of the Incarnation. The marital love of God towards Israel but also towards every person, is carried out in the Incarnation in a way which goes beyond the measure of people's expectations. We discover this in the Annunciation passage where the New Covenant becomes known as the Covenant of God's marriage with mankind, of divinity with humanity, in the light of the marital covenant. Mary the Virgin of Nazareth is the pre-eminent "virgin-Israel of the prophet Jeremiah. In her the marital love of God announced by the prophets is perfectly and definitively focused. She is also that virgin spouse to whom it is granted to conceive and bear the Son of God; the special fruit of God's marital love towards humanity which is represented by and almost summarized in Mary.

The Holy Spirit, who comes down upon Mary during the Annunciation, is the one who, in the Trinity's relationship, expresses in his Person the marital love of God, the 'eternal' love. In the mystery of the Incarnation, in the human conception of God's Son, the Holy Spirit maintains divine transcendence. Luke's text expresses that in a precise way. The nuptial quality of God's love has a completely spiritual and supernatural character. What John will say regarding the believers in Christ is valid all the more for the Son of God who was conceived in the womb of the Virgin 'not by natural generation, nor by human choice, nor by man's decision, but of God' (Jn 1:13). But it especially expresses the supreme union in love, brought about between God and a human being by the power of the Holy Spirit.

In the divine marriage with humanity Mary answers the angel's announcement with the love of a spouse who is able to respond and to adjust to the divine choice in a perfect way. For this reason, especially since St Francis of Assisi's time, the Church calls her the 'spouse of the Holy Spirit.' Only this perfect marital love, deeply rooted in her total self-gift to God, could have brought it about that Mary became the 'Mother of God' in a conscious and worthy fashion through the mystery of the Incarnation.

In the Encyclical *Redemptoris Mater* I wrote: 'The Holy Spirit had already come down upon her and she became his faithful Spouse at the Annunciation, welcoming the Word of the true God, offering 'the full submission of intellect and will.. and freely assenting to the truth revealed by him', indeed abandoning herself totally to God through the 'obedience of faith' whereby she replied to the angel: 'Behold, I am the handmaid of the Lord, let it be done to me according to your word.'

In Mary's act and gesture, which contrast as a mirror image with Eve's behaviour, she stands out in humanity's spiritual history as the new Spouse, the new Eve, the Mother of the living, as the Doctors and Fathers of the Church will often say. She will be the type and model of the New Covenant as a nuptial union of the Holy Spirit with individuals and with the human community, far beyond the sphere of ancient Israel: the totality of individuals and peoples will be called to receive the gift and become its beneficiary in the new community of believers who have received 'the power to become sons and daughters of God' (Jn 1:12) and in Baptism are born again 'of the Spirit' (Jn 3:6) by entering into and belonging to God's family.

Synods

The Synods, ordinary and extraordinary called by the Pope, are his manner of acting collegially. Some have been notable for the papal documents, Apostolic Exhortations, issued on the basis of their findings. *Catechesi Tradendae*, 4 March, 1979, was a sequel to the Synod on Catechetics held under Paul VI (qv). *Familiaris Consortio*, 22 November, 1981 followed a Synod on the family, *Reconciliatio et Poenitentia* was the sequel to a Synod on this theme. (After the 1987 Synod on the "Vocation and Mission of the Laity in the Church and the World Twenty Years after the Second Vatican Council", the Pope issued on 30 December, 1988 his Apostolic Exhortation, *Christifideles Laici*. Influenced also by the Synod he had earlier, 15 August, published an Apostolic Letter on women in the Church, *Mulieris Dignitatem*.) A very important Synod is being prepared at the present time, on the consecrated, that is, religious life. It will surely be followed by an Apostolic Exhortation. The year also sees the African Synod.

Vassula Rydén (b.1942)

Why introduce one individual into this analytical account of the life and work of the reigning Pope? There are these cogent reasons for doing so. She is a member of the Greek Orthodox Church and the Orthodox are, at the present time, of immediate compelling importance to anyone interested in the revival of religion; since the fall of communism the Orthodox have shown many signs of this revival across the world. John Paul II is aware of this (see article *Orthodox, The*); he knows of the challenge it offers to the Catholic Church, probably knows how this singular witness to Jesus Christ is misrepresented by some of his Catholic priests.

At a time when religious commentators point to the deteriorating relations between the two Churches Vassula Rydén has a captial role. She has a worldwide Catholic constituency, audiences of thousands in large cities of the five continents for the last three years; her writings issued first five years ago are read in twenty-one different languages; eighty thousand copies of the French edition have been sold, fifty-seven thousand of the Portuguese in Brazil alone!

Vassula exemplifies God's frequent choice of converts to convert the world; her conversion, in 1985, was from a life of total religious indifference over thirty years. To a mind totally blank on religion the Lord has given daily a body of theological and spiritual doctrine pre-eminently Catholic. Not only is she the first member of the Orthodox Church in history to exercise a didactic mission towards Catholics. She is the first Orthodox writer to set forth truths which bear close comparison with the teaching of a Pope who is her contemporary. The theological analysis of her writings brings into relief themes like devotion to the Holy Spirit (qv), the Alliance of the Two Hearts (qv), Christian unity, the conversion of Russia (qv), devotion to the Immaculate Heart of Mary, the spreading apostasy, all of which also recur in the teaching of John Paul II. It is unnecessary to stress the Pope's insistence on a correct attitude to the Holy Spirit; it is illustrated in several articles in the present work. In the published writings of Vassula, which is not all that she has written, there are 800 references to the Holy Spirit; some passages will find their way into anthologies, so profound and yet so relevant to the life of the Church and of its members is their content.

More remarkable still is the fact that Vassula is, in the messages she records from Jesus, a defender and protagonist of Pope John Paul II. Some passages must be quoted - the reader will note that when the Lord speaks of "Peter" he is referring to the present Pope:

> How I cry from my cross. Ah Peter. I come to you because I know you remained faithful to me. Oh Peter, look at my Heart...hear my cries, beloved soul. I, the Lord, find no love, no holiness in those Cains; they are many; they have laid desolate my house. On what will my lambs feed since their hands are empty? They have nothing to offer them since they made a desert out of my foundation. Pray Peter and I will lift you so that you will see this wilderness from above, and I will let you penetrate into the wound of my Heart. I will let you see the lance's blade. Your heart will cry out with pain when you will see it. Peter, I will give you the strength and the courage, you will need to have, so that you may pull it out.

That was spoken on 29 March, 1988. On 21 June of the same year Vassula received this message:

> Pray for those souls who oppose Peter; pray for those who are trying to silence Peter. The days are now numbered and my soul is submerged in sorrow; my Sacred Heart is imbued with bitterness; my soul is yearning for them to realize their error. Those who oppose Peter are opposing my Church; they are opposing

my law; they are opposing me, their Lord and God; they are condemning Peter of the Lambs, thus condemning my law. Blinded by vanity himself they do not see clear anymore that by condemning Peter they are not following the law but instead become judges of my own law. O listen to what the Spirit says to the Church. Return, come back beloved one. It is I, the Lord, who have selected Peter; Peter who today bears the name John Paul II. I am telling you, beloved one, my Sacred Heart has chosen him. Come back, reconcile for my sake beloved. I, the Lord, will forgive your sins and will purify you. Return. Return all of you to Peter, for it is I your God who has chosen him; it is I who have given him a disciple's tongue and, through me, he is able to reply to the weary.

On 26 July, 1988 Vassula received this message in the course of a lengthy communication:

Thorns and briars are replacing the lilies and roses I had planted by my own hand; they have choked my flowers and one after another; they have grown with Satan's help to encircle and trap.. My flower (Vassula thought this was John Paul II) they are getting closer daily and are so near now to molest and feel their poisonous sting -those thorns will suffocate him. Peter is trapped and stands helpless in their midst."

Then Our Lady appeared to Vassula, who said, "Yes, Holy Mother." Our Lady answered: "Believe, for all this is happening. My Son's Body will bleed even more profusely. Peter's end is near. Love is missing."

These testimonies are certainly important. This is the first time in nine hundred and forty years that an Orthodox writer has publicly championed the cause of the Roman Pontiff, his universal primacy. This, let us admit it, has been the principal obstacle on the way of unity. About the present Pope Vassula had a special message of which the essential passage must be introduced:

I am addressing you today to tell you from the core of My Heart the same embittered words I uttered at My Last Supper around My disciples: 'someone who shares My table rebels against Me.' I tell you this now, before it happens, so that when it does happen you may believe that I am He speaking, today.

My little children, do not let your hearts be troubled, trust in Me and do not fear. Soon a Baptism of Fire will be sent by the Father to burn the crimes of this world. The hour will come when men of power will enter My Sanctuary, men who do not come from Me; in fact this hour is already here. I, Jesus Christ, wish to warn My priests, bishops and cardinals, I wish to warn all My House of a great tribulation. My Church is approaching a great tribulation. Remember, I have chosen you by My sanctifying Spirit to glorify Me; I have chosen you from the beginning to be the sturdy pillars of My Church and to live by faith in the Truth; I have chosen you to share My Glory and to shepherd My lambs. I tell you solemnly that you will soon be tested by fire. Pray and fast so as not to be put to the test; stand firm and **keep** the traditions you were taught. **Obey My Pope no matter what comes up**. Remain faithful to him and I will give you the graces and the strength you will need. I urge you to **keep faithful to him** and keep away from anyone who rebels against him. Above all, **never listen to anyone who dispels him**; never let your love for him grow insincere.

Soon you will be faced with an ordeal as you have never experienced before. My enemies will try to buy you for themselves with insidious speeches - the evil one is at his work already and Destruction is not far away from you. The pope will have much to suffer - this is why you will all be persecuted for proclaiming the Truth and for being obedient to My pope.

Vatican II

Karol Wojtyla was on 4 July, 1958, when he was little over thirty-eight years of age, named to the titular See of Ombi and appointed Auxiliary Bishop of Cracow, one of the last nominations of Pius XII. On 17 May he was elected Vicar Capitular or acting Archbishop of Cracow. On 30 December, Paul VI (qv) named him Archbishop Metropolitan of the historic diocese. He attended Vatican II from its first session until the end.

One of the experts attending the Council, Henri de Lubac, SJ, later Cardinal, has, in a famous interview to which *France Catholique* devoted on one occasion its entire space, recalled that he was so impressed by the young Polish bishop that he saw him as a possible future Pope. The Polish hierarchy were happy to have as their spokesman one with valid credentials. This was a man not overawed by the vast assembly and all the conciliar paraphernalia. He was not cowed or bewitched by the army of experts who flocked to Rome to keep the intellectual pot simmering, if not on the boil. He was not to be patronised by any of them, for he was their equal. He could face new problems without panic. If people talked to him about religious freedom, he knew what tyranny was, how Nazis and communists operated. To scholarly, slightly remote talk about the People of God, laboratory language in some cases, he could oppose the experience of a nation which was actively, wholeheartedly part of the people of God, and willing to pay the price for their allegiance. It took a strong mind and an independent spirit to separate, in those exciting times, durable gains from ephemera.

The future Pope's links with the Council may be studied under these aspects: his active co-operation in the sessions, his efforts to make the teaching meaningful in the lives of his diocesan faithful, his fidelity to the Council since he became Pope. During the Council sessions Bishop Wojtyla first supported the joint request made by the Polish hierarchy that the Pope, John XXIII, later Paul VI, publicly consecrate the world to the Immaculate Heart of Mary, Mother of the Church, in union with the entire college of bishops. Paul VI thought that he had given satisfaction to this collective desire by his proclamation of Mary, Mother of the Church, 21 November, 1964. Not quite!

During the conciliar sessions Bishop Wojtyla spoke eleven times. His contributions were principally on the subject of divine revelation; briefly, on religious liberty; on the apostolate of the laity; on Christian marriage; on the Church in the modern world; on atheism - here he was really informative to the Council Fathers. More important was his work published after the sessions of Vatican II to explain its findings, teaching and relevance to the faithful: *Foundations of Renewal, A Treatise on the Implementation of Vatican II*, 366 pages. Has any other bishop published such a work, so complete a work on the Council?

Has the Pope been faithful to the Council? Every important document which he has issued carries abundant references to the conciliar texts. The *Catechism of the Catholic Church* (qv) was not his personal composition, but it was written with respect to his views. The index of references to Council documents takes more than four two column pages.

John Paul II has implemented the teaching of the Council in regard to synods. He has fostered the local church throughout the world by his travels. He has been steadfast in his witness to the integral doctrine of the Church.

Veritatis Splendor (6 August, 1993)

This is Pope John Paul's statement on the objective moral order, his reply to the relativism which subtly or overtly has been undermining some moral teaching. The tone of the Encyclical is not merely condemnatory, asking for witch-hunts, but explanatory, calling for reflection and review of present-day theories, where they need such a review. The Encyclical was being prepared for a number of years, was, on the word of Cardinal Ratzinger (qv) the object of wide consultation. The Cardinal certainly influenced its contents, as, apparently, did a Polish friend of the Pope's, professor Fr Szostek of Lublin University. The Encyclical was ready before the *Catechism of the Catholic Church* (qv) but it was thought better to allow the latter work to appear first. Together they constitute a monument of the pontificate.

The Encyclical was leaked at least partially before official publication, which led to total misrepresentation, as the very brief sections dealing with sexuality were taken as the substance of the document; they are just incidental. The Press (qv) seemed to lose interest when this fact was evident. Since, with reservations, the advertising dictum may be quoted "all publicity is good publicity", the media interest, fragmentary and misguided though it was, may benefit diffusion of the papal text. So will the fact of sustained commentary by different authors in the Catholic press, the London based *Tablet* for instance; the articles are now appearing as a book.

Reactions were predictable. Apart from what Hans Urs von Balthasar called the "Anti-Roman complex" those opposed to John Paul II and those, like the present writer, utterly loyal to him, are known. But even from the diehard critics few would have expected such a stricture as is expressed in the word "dictator." We live and learn. A man who attacked the Pope on the basis of his national origin, will presumably say something extreme when the Pope defies popular trends.

What the attentive reader will need to consider is the illuminating link between coherent ethical theory and the problem put to the Lord himself while in the course of his ministry. Equally stimulating is the consideration of present day moral theories, on the fundamental option, consequentialism and proportionalism. These intellectual positions are dealt with sympathetically. The overriding thesis of the Encyclical is maintained: certain acts are intrinsically wrong. There is, also, a wealth of reflection on key concepts in Christian ethical philosophy, conscience, freedom, natural law. Moral theologians are invited to pursue reflection on these and other matters raised. Already from those really qualified there has been a positive response, recognition that authoritative teaching does not nullify thorough research.

Reading of the Encyclical could profitably be supplemented by study of the series of talks given by the Pope on the nature, kinds and effects of sin, during 1986.

Youth and John Paul II

The Pope has been willing to speak especially to young audiences at different times in his pontificate. He sent a written message to Dutch youth; spoke in dialogue with French youth in the Parc des Princes, spoke also to Mexican youth on the occasion of his second visit to their country in 1990. But his personal innovation has been World Youth Day. Its evolution began in 1984 when tens of thousands of young people from forty different countries answered the Pope's invitation to meet him in the Vatican during the four days that ended on 15 April, Palm Sunday, the conclusion of the Church's Holy Year of Reconciliation. On Palm Sunday, the following year, 31 March, 250,000 young people met the Pope in St Peter's Square; this time it was in harmony with the United Nations "International Year of Youth", the theme being peace and unity. That day week, Easter Sunday, the Pope proposed annual World Youth Day gatherings. On 22 January following, a Vatican statement made it clear that the Pope hoped for an annual day for youth, to be celebrated in dioceses on Palm Sunday - or another day for pastoral reasons - under the direction of the Pontifical Council for the Laity. It was stressed by the latter that the Church wished to show her unity with youth "in their anxieties and concerns, their efforts and hopes... to respond by transmitting to them the certainty, truth and love which is Christ."

The first World Youth Day was held in Buenos Aires, 11-12 April, 1987. Those who came from Latin America, Europe and Africa may have been one million. It was the first time, in modern history, that a Pope celebrated Palm Sunday outside the Vatican. The theme was "We ourselves have known and put our faith in God's love toward us." (1 Jn 1:3)

In 1989 the venue was the shrine of Santiago de Compostella, centre of one of the great medieval pilgrimages. The theme was "Christ the Way, the Truth and the Life" (Jn 14:6). The time was changed to 16-20 August; 600,000 participants were with the Holy Father. In 1991 Czestochowa, in the Pope's homeland, welcomed one million and a half young people, from 11-15 August. The theme was "You have received a spirit of sonship" (Rom 8:15). The event was memorable because it was the first time that young people from the East European countries attended a Church-sponsored international assembly.

In 1993 Denver, Colorado, was the scene. Gloomy forecasts were about beforehand. In fact it was a triumph. The Pope spoke movingly on a favourite subject, on the feast of Our Lady's Assumption. He said, among other things:

> The Eighth World Youth Day is a celebration of life. This gathering has been the occasion of a serious reflection on the words of Jesus Christ: 'I came that they may have life and have it abundantly' (Jn 10:10). Young people from every corner of the world, in ardent prayer you have opened your hearts to the truth of Christ's promise of new life. Through the sacraments, especially Penance and the Eucharist, and by means of the unity and friendship created among so many, you have had a real and transforming experience of the new life which only Christ can give. You, young pilgrims, have also shown that you understand that Christ's gift is not for you alone. You have become more conscious of your vocation and mission in the Church and in the world. For me, our meeting has been a deep and moving experience of your faith in Christ, and I make my own the words of St Paul: 'I have great confidence in you, I have great pride in you. I am filled with encouragement. I am overflowing with joy.' (2 Cor 7:4)

Manifest in all these ceremonies is the absence of gimmicks; central the Person of Christ. Next World Youth Day is scheduled for Manila, in the land of the Two Hearts, 1995.

APPENDIX I

Rev. Michael O'Carroll, C.S.Sp. Brief Curriculum Vitae and Outline Bibliography.

C.V.

Education: Blackrock College, Dublin; University College Dublin (B.A. Philosophy; H.Dip. Education) Fribourg University (D.D. Dissertation: Spiritual Direction according to Ven. Francis Libermann, 1939).

Career:

Education: Professor Blackrock College (Religious Knowledge, History, French Language and Literature);

Journalism: *Catholic Standard* (14 years sole editorial writer, Features especially on Vatican II in session, book reviews); *The Leader* (10 years identical service); much occasional work elsewhere;

Pastoral Ministry: *Lay Apostolate*, chaplain to College Scout Troop; Spiritual Director three praesidia Legion of Mary; Adult Education courses in Social Science and Practical Psychology, Dun Laoghaire Technical College; chaplain annually to Irish Handicapped, Banneux Shrine; care of adopted children;

Spiritual Training: Retreats and lectures; chaplain Blackrock Carmelite Convent;

Ecclesial Collaboration: Deep cultural and intellectual attachment to the Church in France with diocesan service (Beauvais) annually for twenty years;

Ecumenism: Member of the Mercier Society (1941-1944) for dialogue with Protestants, and of the wartime Pillar of Fire Society for dialogue with Jews; first chairman of Irish branch of the Ecumenical Society of the Blessed Virgin May;

Recognition: Elected to General chapters C.S.Sp., 1968 (continued to 1969), 1974; Member of the Pontifical Marian Academy; *Associé des Bollandistes*; Member of the French Society of Marian Studies.

BIBLIOGRAPHY

1. Articles in religious periodicals e.g. The Irish Rosary, Missionary Annals of the Holy Ghost Fathers, Blackrock College Annual, *Maria Legionis* (organ of the Legion of Mary), Hibernia, Madonna, Knock Shrine Annual;

2. Articles in theological reviews, Clergy Review, Homiletic and Pastoral Review, Irish Ecclesiastical Record, Irish Theological Quarterly, The Furrow, Doctrine and Life, *Marianum, Ephemerides Mariologicae*; prefaces to a number of books;

3. Contributions: International Mariological Congresses, Rome, Saragossa, Malta, Kevalaer, Huelva; dictionaries, *Dictionnaire de Spiritualité* (25 articles); Marienlexikon (Regensburg) (24 articles written or requested) Modern Dictionary of Theology (1 article) Encyclopedia of Catholic Practice (12 articles); commemorative volumes: Dom Columba Marmion, Fr. René Laurentin, Fr. G.M. Besutti, O.S.M.; Fr. Theodore Koechler, S.M.; Professor Heinrich Beck (Bamberg);

4. Five pamphlets, Ven. Francis Libermann (2), The secret of Knock, African Glory (Mgr. Alexander Le Roy), Disciples of St. Thérèse of Lisieux, Lourdes Centenary Year.

Books: twenty on Marian theology, hagiography and the Papacy, among which: *Joseph, Son of David; Mediatress of All Graces; Medjugorje, Facts, Documents, Theology; Le Sanctuaire de Knock* (awaiting publication in Paris); *Pius XII, Greatness Dishonoured - A documented Study*; five theological encyclopedias, *Theotokos* (Our Lady), *Trinitas* (the Holy Trinity), *Corpus Christi* (the Eucharist), *Veni Creator Spiritus* (the Holy Spirit), *Verbum Caro* (Jesus the Christ); *John Paul II, A Dictionary of His Life and Teachings; Vassula of the Sacred Heart's Passion; Bearer of the Light - Vassula, Mediatrix of Divided Christians:*

APPENDIX II

CONTENTS

NEW TITLES AVAILABLE

John Paul II - A Dictionary of His Life and Teachings by M O'Carroll CSSp
A quick and fascinating guide to the life and teachings of this outstanding leader of the Church, which will be of great help to Catholics in these confused times. What has he said about the third secret of Fatima? What does the Pope think of Opus Dei? the Orthodox Churches? the Jews? What was his relationship with Monsignor Lefebvre? All these questions have been answered by this comprehensive dictionary, compiled by one of the outstanding theologians of our day, Father Michael O'Carroll CSSp.

Bearer of the Light by M O'Carroll CSSp
This is the second book by Father Michael O'Carroll on Vassula and the messages 'True Life in God.' In this book Vassula's most recent visit to Russia is recorded. Other themes include: pre-history of her conversion; extraordinary signs; the Passion; Chastisement and Purification. The book includes some extraordinary personal testimonies from people all around the world who experienced supernatural events in her presence. A must for any reader of the 'True Life in God' messages.

Volume IV (Notebooks 65-71)
This most recent volume of the messages of 'True Life in God' contains, among other things: prophecies on Russia explained - resurrection of the Church - repairing what was undone - unity by intermarriage. Daniel explained - the Rebel - the "enemy enthroning himself in 'my sanctuary'" - abolition of the Perpetual Sacrifice. Message to Cardinals, bishops and priests (17 March 1993).

Fire of Love
In this book prepared by Vassula Rydén as a gift to her spiritual advisor Michael O'Carroll CSSP, she selects from the complete writings to date of 'True Life in God' what she considers the most important references to the Holy Spirit. This book will be of interest to any reader with devotion to the Holy Spirit.

When God Gives a Sign by René Laurentin
Father Laurentin has long been recognised for his scientific and theological approach to claimed apparitions and his search for the truth. In this book he skillfully and with discernment answers questions arising in relation to Vassula Rydén's charism and the 'True Life in God' messages.
(This book is available in the UK from Sue Ellis, Spring House, Spring Bottom Lane, Bletchingly, Surrey, England Tel: 0883 346365 and in the USA from Trinitas, PO Box 475, Independence, MO, USA 64051)

OTHER TITLES AVAILABLE

Volume I (Notebooks 1-31)

Guardian angel Daniel, prepares Vassula to meet Jesus. Jesus teaches Vassula love of God, the scriptures; describes His passion; His love of 'daughter' Russia and its resurrection; the Great Apostasy. He links Garabandal to Fatima; His desire for unity of the Churches.

Volume II (Notebooks 32-58)

Jesus teaches that God is alive and very near, desiring a return to love, Adoration, sharing His Passion, consoling Him; return of Jesus. He teaches about the state of the Church, His shepherds; the renewal of His vineyards; Devotion to the Two Sacred Hearts of Jesus and Mary; expands on the ten commandments and Beatitudes; Apocalypse 12. The rebellion in the Church and the Great Apostasy; the suffering of His Peter; the minature judgement; unrolling of the 'scrolls.' Many prayers, of consecration, of adoration, of consolation, praise etc... to Father, Son and Holy Spirit.

Volume III (Notebooks 59-64)

Among the contents in this volume: Jesus marks foreheads with the consecration to him, Judgement Day, the time of sorting, the lamb's seal, the three days of darkness, and a strong message when the earth will shake and the sky will vanish.

Prayers of Jesus and Vassula

A beautiful assortment of prayers, some given by Jesus, others by Vassula, inspired by the Holy Spirit. A section on the Devotion to the Two Hearts; Daily Prayers and quotations of Jesus' teaching how to pray.

Vassula of the Sacred Heart's Passion by Michael O'Carroll C.S.Sp.

A 220 page book giving an outline of Vassula's life, her charism and analysis of Jesus' messages in the light of the teaching of the Church. Also a message to cardinals, bishops and priests of 'The Rebel' with a warning not to listen or follow the teaching of anyone except the Holy Father, John Paul II. (17 March 1993)

NATIONAL DISTRIBUTORS (ENGLISH EDITION)

United Kingdom

Chris Lynch
JMJ Publications
PO Box 385
Belfast BT9 6RQ
Northern Ireland
Tel: (232) 381596
Fax: (232) 381596

Australia

Center for Peace
c/o Leon LeGrand
91 Auburn Road
AUBURN Victoria
Australia 3123
Fax: (03) 882-9675
Tel: (03) 882-9822

United States

John Lynch
319 North Virginia Ave
North Massapequa
N.Y.
USA 11758
Fax: (516) 293-9635
Tel: (516) 293-9635

Canada

Caravan Agencies Ltd
6 Dumbarton Blvd
Winnipeg
Manitoba
Canada R3P 2C4
Fax: (204) 895 8878
Tel: (204) 895 7544

South Africa

Winnie Williams
Friends of Medjugorje
PO Box 32817
Braamfontein 2017
Johannesburg
South Africa
Tel: (011) 640-6583
Fax: (011) 339-7185

Republic of Ireland

D.M.Publications
"Maryville"
Loughshinney
Skerries
Co Dublin

Tel: (1) 8491458

Malawi

Rui Francisco
PO Box 124
Lilongwe
Malawi
Africa

Fax: (265) 721504

<u>Denmark</u>: Niels Huidt, Mysundegade 8V, DK 1668, Copenhagen V, Denmark (Fax: 45 331 33115)

<u>Switzerland</u>: Parvis, CH-1648, Hautville, Switzerland (Tel: 41 29 51905)

<u>Holland</u>: Stichting Getuigenis, Jan Van Hooffstraat 8, 5611 ED Eindhoven, Holland (Tel: 040 43 39 89 Fax: 040 44 02 74)

<u>Queries relating to any version, please contact</u>:

'True Life in God', PO Box 902, CH-1800 Vevey, Switzerland